JACOB AND EGYPT

The Sovereignty of God

JOHN MACARTHUR

THOMAS NELSON
Since 1798

Published in Nashville, Tennessee, by Thomas Nelson. Thomas Nelson is a trademark of Thomas Nelson, Inc.

Layout, design, and writing assistance by Gregory C. Benoit Publishing, Old Mystic, CT. G̶B

Thomas Nelson, Inc. titles may be purchased in bulk for educational, business, fund-raising, or sales promotional use. For information, please e-mail *SpecialMarkets@ThomasNelson.com*.

Scripture quotations are taken from THE NEW KING JAMES VERSION. Copyright © 1982 by Thomas Nelson, Inc. Used by permission. All rights reserved.

ISBN 978-1-4185-3324-3

Printed in the United States of America

08 09 10 11 12 RRD 5 4 3 2 1

CONTENTS

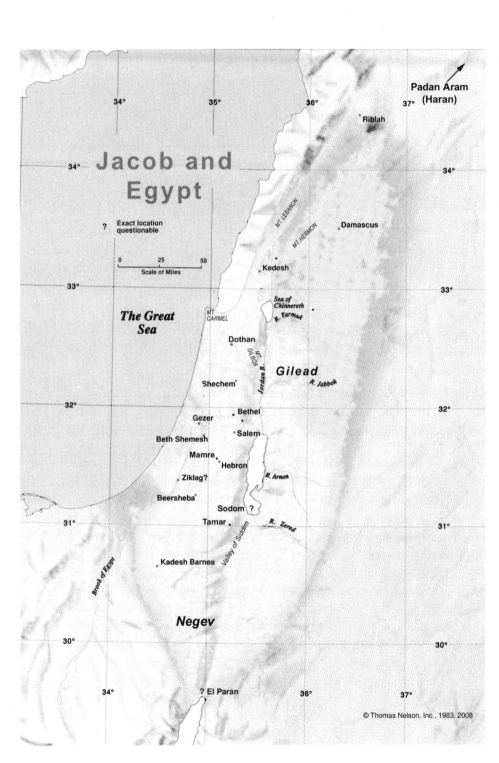

Jacob and Egypt

? Exact location questionable

0   25   50
Scale of Miles

The Great Sea

Padan Aram (Haran)

Riblah

MT. LEBANON

MT. HERMON

Damascus

Kedesh

Sea of Chinnereth

R. Yarmuk

MT. CARMEL

Dothan

MT. GILBOA

Jordan R.

Gilead

Shechem

R. Jabbok

Bethel

Gezer

Salem

Beth Shemesh

Mamre

Hebron

Ziklag?

R. Arnon

Beersheba

Sodom ?

Tamar

R. Zered

Valley of Siddim

Kadesh Barnea

Brook of Egypt

Negev

? El Paran

© Thomas Nelson, Inc., 1983, 2008

INTRODUCTION

Jacob, also called Israel, had twelve sons and one daughter. The book of Genesis gives us many vignettes from the lives of these people. Each was a very real human being, made of the same flesh as you and me, and with similar strengths and weaknesses. They each faced unique trials and temptations. One was raped; another was sold into slavery; yet another was faced with the death of two sons. Some of these characters responded by trusting in God's faithfulness alone; others took revenge into their own hands. But one lesson emerges from all these stories: God is in control of all things! Even when it seemed He was nowhere to be found, He was, in fact, carefully guiding the events in these characters' lives. They did, after all, become the mighty nation of Israel.

This does not mean they lived *sinless* lives—quite the opposite, in some cases. Nevertheless, God was at work in them, even when they were living in sin, to bring about His plans for His people. What were His plans? Reconciliation in the family of Jacob—and in the lives of His people throughout the ages: it was through Jacob's family that Christ was born.

In these twelve studies, we will jump back and forth in chronological history, looking at one historical period, then skipping forward or backward in time as needed. We will examine Joseph's example of a servant, then study how the same man became the model of a godly leader. We will witness Judah grow from a self-serving sinner into a qualified leader in his family—who was ultimately included in the genealogy of Jesus. And best of all, we will learn some precious truths about the character of God, and we will see His great faithfulness in keeping His promises. We will learn, in short, what it means to walk by faith.

ᕗ WHAT WE'LL BE STUDYING ᕘ

This study guide is divided into four distinct sections in which we will examine selected Bible passages:

SECTION 1: HISTORY. In this first section, we will focus on the historical setting of our Bible text. These five lessons will give a broad overview of the people, places, and events that are important to this study. They will also provide the background for the next two sections. This is our most purely historical segment, focusing simply on what happened and why.

Section 2: Characters. The four lessons in this section will give us an opportunity to zoom in on the characters from our Scripture passages. Some of these people were introduced in section 1, but in this part of the study guide we will take a much closer look at these personalities. Why did God see fit to include them in His Book in the first place? What made them unique? What can we learn from their lives? In this practical section, we will answer all of these questions and more, as we learn how to live wisely by emulating the wisdom of those who came before us.

Section 3: Themes. Section 3 consists of two lessons in which we will consider some of the broader themes and doctrines touched on in our selected Scripture passages. This is the guide's most abstract portion, wherein we will ponder specific doctrinal and theological questions that are important to the church today. As we ask what these truths mean to us as Christians, we will also look for practical ways to base our lives upon God's truth.

Section 4: Summary. In our final section, we will look back at the principles that we have discovered in the scriptures throughout this study guide. These will be our "take-away" principles, those which permeate the Bible passages that we have studied. As always, we will be looking for ways to make these truths a part of our everyday lives.

~ About the Lessons ~

⇥ Each study begins with an introduction that provides the background for the selected Scripture passages.

⇥ To assist you in your reading, a section of notes—a miniature Bible commentary of sorts—offers both cultural information and additional insights.

⇥ A series of questions is provided to help you dig a bit deeper into the Bible text.

⇥ Overriding principles brought to light by the Bible text will be studied in each lesson. These principles summarize a variety of doctrines and practical truths found throughout the Bible.

⇥ Finally, additional questions will help you mine the deep riches of God's Word and, most importantly, to apply those truths to your own life.

Section i:

History

In This Section:

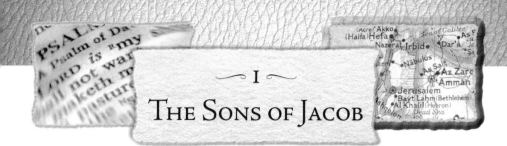

～ I ～
THE SONS OF JACOB

GENESIS 35, 37

～ HISTORICAL BACKGROUND ～

Our study opens with Jacob and his twelve sons living in Canaan at Bethel. (See the map in the Introduction.) Jacob, also called Israel, had two wives and two concubines who bore him sons. It will be important to understand the background of this family arrangement as we proceed in our studies.

Jacob had spent many years working for his uncle Laban, and during that time he had fallen in love with Laban's younger daughter, Rachel. He asked Laban for permission to marry Rachel, and Laban agreed—on one condition: Jacob would work for seven years to earn her hand. Jacob readily agreed to this condition, but at the end of the seven years, Laban tricked him by giving him his older daughter, Leah, instead of Rachel. Jacob then worked for another seven years to earn the hand of Rachel.

As time went along, Jacob loved Rachel more than Leah and made no effort to disguise the fact. This must have caused Leah deep grief, but the Lord comforted her by giving her six sons, while Rachel remained barren. Rachel, in turn, became jealous of her sister's fertility, and she persuaded Jacob to produce children through her maidservant. (The maidservant's children would have been viewed as being Rachel's.) Leah responded as though it were a competition, and she gave Jacob *her* maidservant as well. This competition continued between the two sisters, and Leah had another two sons and a daughter in the process—while Rachel had none.

Rachel eventually cried out to the Lord in her grief, and He showed His mercy and opened her womb. She gave birth to Joseph and later to Benjamin. Jacob eventually had a total of twelve sons, as well as at least one daughter. (We will look at her in Study 2.)

Jacob took great delight in his son Joseph, because not only had he been born through his beloved wife Rachel, but he was also born late in Jacob's life. This led to Jacob playing favorites among his sons, loving Joseph and Benjamin more openly than he did his other ten sons. Needless to say, Jacob's older sons came to resent their younger brother Joseph.

All of this favoritism and competition and resentment led to a household that lacked peace and unity. As our study opens, Jacob's sons are mostly grown men with families of their own, and Joseph is seventeen. The tensions among the brothers are about to come to a head.

⤳ READING GENESIS 35:22–29 ⤶

MY TWELVE SONS: *Jacob had twelve sons through four different women, as well as several daughters.*

22. REUBEN WENT AND LAY WITH BILHAH: Reuben was Jacob's firstborn son, born through Leah; Bilhah was Rachel's maidservant. This grievous sin cost Reuben his birthright and his status as firstborn, as we will see in the following passages. There is an irony here, however, in the loss of the birthright: Jacob himself had swindled the birthright from his twin brother, Esau, many years before (Genesis 25).

23. LEAH: Leah was the older daughter of Laban, Jacob's uncle. "Leah's eyes were delicate, but Rachel was beautiful of form and appearance" (Genesis 29:17). The exact meaning of this is unclear, but it is clear that in Jacob's opinion, Leah was not as physically attractive as Rachel.

LEVI: The descendants of Levi would eventually become the only men eligible for the priesthood in Israel.

JUDAH: David would be a descendant of Judah—and ultimately so would Jesus Himself. We will look more closely at Judah in Study 7.

24. RACHEL: Jacob loved Rachel (Genesis 29:18), the younger sister of Leah. But Jacob's youth had been characterized by treachery and deceit (see book two in this series, *The Father of Israel*, for studies on Jacob's life), so it should come as no surprise that his uncle Laban was also treacherous and deceitful: he tricked Jacob into marrying Rachel's older sister first. Throughout the remainder of his life, Jacob loved Rachel more than Leah.

BENJAMIN: Rachel died while giving birth to Benjamin (35:16–19), Jacob's final son. She had named him Ben-Oni, meaning "Son of My Sorrow," but Jacob changed it to Benjamin, meaning "Son of the Right Hand." Jacob was more than one hundred years old at the time of Benjamin's birth.

26. PADAN ARAM: This region was many days to the northeast of where Isaac was living. It is also where Abram was living when God called him to Canaan. See Genesis 12 and map in the Introduction.

27. MAMRE: This location was very important in Abraham's life, for example, when he met God face to face and interceded for Sodom and Gomorrah.

⤳ Reading Genesis 37:1–36 ⤲

Tensions Begin to Build: *Jacob had played favorites among his wives; unsurprisingly, he did the same with his sons. His favoritism toward Joseph produced problems.*

1. where his father was a stranger: God had commanded Abraham, Jacob's grandfather, to move to Canaan so that his descendants could inherit the entire land. But Abraham himself had lived as a pilgrim in the land God had promised him, and had died without actually seeing the fulfillment of God's promise. The same was true of Isaac, and would eventually be the case for Jacob. "By faith Abraham obeyed when he was called to go out to the place which he would receive as an inheritance . . . By faith he dwelt in the land of promise as in a foreign country, dwelling in tents with Isaac and Jacob, the heirs with him of the same promise; for he waited for the city which has foundations, whose builder and maker is God" (Hebrews 11:8–10).

2. Joseph brought a bad report: We are not told whether this report was the result of Jacob's questioning his son, or Joseph voluntarily bearing the report to his father. We also do not know what the report was about, so it is difficult to assess Joseph's actions here. Some have suggested that he was spiritually proud or self-righteous, but these conclusions are not supported by what we know. The important element of this verse is that Joseph's brothers resented him, and their resentment had reached the breaking point.

3. Israel loved Joseph more than all his children: There is a sad irony in this favoritism, because Jacob (Israel) himself had grown up with parents who played favorites—his father favored Esau, his mother favored him. This in part led to the permanent separation of Jacob from his brother, Esau, and it led to division and attempted murder among his own children.

he was the son of his old age: Jacob was probably in his nineties when Joseph was born.

tunic of many colors: The meaning of this phrase is uncertain. It may simply refer to a robe with long sleeves. Whatever its distinguishing features, this cloak signified his father's favor (1 Samuel 13:18) and perhaps also some level of authority over his brothers.

4. they hated him: From a human perspective, this is the natural result of a father choosing favorites among his children. This animosity was also modeled by the parents themselves, as there was deep resentment and jealousy between Jacob's wives. Nevertheless, a person is never justified in the eyes of God when he hates his brothers. The sons of Jacob were following in the footsteps of Cain. "Sin lies at the door," the Lord had warned him, "and its desire is for you, but you should rule over it" (Genesis 4:7).

THAT DREAMER OF DREAMS: *God gave Joseph prophetic dreams concerning the future, but this only served to increase his brothers' resentment.*

5–11: The Lord gave Joseph a series of dreams, predicting that he would one day rule over his entire family. This served merely to deepen his brothers' resentment. In their eyes, he was being presumptuous and arrogant, and their own predisposition to resent him led them into further sin. A proper brotherly love toward Joseph would have led his family to rejoice in the Lord's favor toward him. (We will look more closely at these dreams in Study 6.)

12. SHECHEM: Located about fifty miles north of Mamre. See map.

13. ISRAEL: Genesis alternates between "Israel" and "Jacob" to refer to Joseph's father.

18. WHEN THEY SAW HIM AFAR OFF: Compare the parable of Jesus in Luke 20:9–16, which bears striking similarities to this passage.

THEY CONSPIRED AGAINST HIM TO KILL HIM: The brothers were carrying out the sin of Cain, who murdered his own brother because Abel's offering was acceptable to the Lord, while Cain's was rejected. Jacob's sons had been stirred to hatred of their brother because of his prophetic dreams and their father's preference, so, as with Cain, this would have been premeditated murder, not accidental manslaughter or even a momentary passion.

19. THIS DREAMER: The brothers revealed here that they deeply resented Joseph's dreams. It may well be that they resented God's favor toward Joseph in the same way that they resented Jacob's favoritism. Yet God's favor toward an individual has nothing in common with a parent's unfair favoritism, for God does not choose favorites (Acts 10:34)—all men and women stand equal before Him, justified only by His Son's blood.

PLOTTING MURDER: *Joseph had gone out to find his brothers in the fields, but they saw him coming and plotted his death. But one brother tried to save him.*

20. LET US NOW KILL HIM: The sons of Jacob meant exactly what they said: it was their deliberate intention to murder their brother Joseph. We will see that God used their wicked plans for His good purposes, but we must not overlook the fact that Joseph's brothers fully intended to kill him.

WHAT WILL BECOME OF HIS DREAMS: If you recall, the Lord had asked Cain, "Why are you angry? And why has your countenance fallen? If you do well, will you not be accepted?" (Genesis 4:6–7). Joseph's brothers had the same opportunities to serve God and be used by Him that Joseph had, but their own anger and resentment was preventing them. What's worse, they thought they could somehow short-circuit God's plans by murdering Joseph—but God's plans cannot be thwarted.

21. Reuben: Reuben was Jacob's firstborn son and the rightful heir to the birthright. He had committed a grievous sin against his father (35:22), however, and would eventually lose that birthright. This same situation occurred in Jacob's life, when his older twin brother, Esau, sold his birthright for a bowl of stew (Genesis 25). Nevertheless, at this point Reuben seemed to be taking his role as firstborn seriously; he was the only one of the brothers who attempted to save Joseph's life.

23. THEY STRIPPED JOSEPH OF HIS TUNIC: The brothers' attitude was one of angry vengeance. They had already expressed their desire to prevent Joseph's prophetic dreams from coming to fulfillment, and now they hoped to spite their father's favoritism. There was also a grim pragmatism in this gesture, as they intended to use the tunic to hide their crime.

24. CAST HIM INTO A PIT: There are interesting parallels between this experience and what Joseph will later suffer in Egypt, as Potiphar's wife strips him of his cloak and he is thrown into the pit of prison.

SOLD INTO SLAVERY: *Joseph's hard-hearted brothers have agreed not to murder him, but that does not mean that they will let him return home. There is a more profitable way.*

25. THEY SAT DOWN TO EAT A MEAL: What a picture of cold-hearted ruthlessness! Joseph's brothers had set out to murder their own flesh and blood, yet their consciences did not bother them in the least; they were content to sit at the mouth of the pit and eat lunch, probably hearing the pleas of Joseph all the while.

A COMPANY OF ISHMAELITES: This caravan was composed of Midianites (v. 28) as well as Ishmaelites. The Midianites were descended from Abraham and Keturah (Genesis 25:1–2), and the Ishmaelites were descended from Abraham and Hagar (Genesis 16). These traders, therefore, were actually distant cousins of Joseph and his brothers.

26. WHAT PROFIT IS THERE . . . ?: Judah's words seemed to indicate that the brothers were undecided about what to do with Joseph. Reuben intended to take Joseph safely home, but he had evidently gone off at this point to tend sheep. The remaining brothers still had no intention of taking Joseph home. It is very sad that the closest they came to showing mercy was when it might bring a profit.

27. HE IS OUR BROTHER AND OUR FLESH: It is possible that Judah was sincerely trying to save Joseph's life; it is equally possible that he was being self-righteous in this sentiment. Either way, he later came to recognize that he was as responsible as anyone for the treachery done to his flesh and blood.

HIS BROTHERS LISTENED: Reuben's leadership had proven completely ineffective in this whole episode because he had already lost his position as the firstborn son in God's eyes, due to his wicked sin against his father. Interestingly, in contrast, Judah was already developing as the leader of his brothers—even though that leadership was toward evil at this point. Judah later received the rights of the firstborn; we will look at him more closely in Study 7.

29. REUBEN RETURNED TO THE PIT: Reuben's intentions were good, but his earlier sin (35:22) had caused his rights as firstborn to be removed from him—and thus he had lost effectiveness as the leader of his brothers.

30. WHERE SHALL I GO?: Reuben will provide us with a good contrast to Judah in their respective responses to similar situations. Reuben's response here was certainly one of grief and sorrow, yet the focus was still on himself. Judah would later respond to Benjamin's danger by worrying about its effect on his father.

31. KILLED A KID OF THE GOATS: This blood would soon deceive Jacob into believing that his beloved son was dead. Here we find another irony that dated back to Jacob's own life, when he killed a kid and used its skin to deceive his father, Isaac (Genesis 27), pretending to be Isaac's favorite son, Esau.

↳ FIRST IMPRESSIONS ↰

1. Where did the competition and resentment originate among the twelve sons? Why did they hate Joseph in particular?

2. What, if anything, did Joseph do to make his troubles worse? In what ways was he completely innocent?

3. Put yourself in Joseph's place. What would you have been thinking as you sat at the bottom of the pit? How would you have responded to your brothers? To God?

4. It was actually God's plan for Joseph to go into Egypt. List specific ways in which God was leading these events behind the scenes.

⤙ Some Key Principles ⤚

God is in control of all our circumstances, even when things seem to be going wrong.

The Lord had told Abraham, many years before these events, that his descendants would go into Egypt for four hundred years (Genesis 15:13–14). It was His plan from the beginning that Joseph should lead his family into Egypt, and the events in these passages were part of that plan.

But the hand of God was not readily apparent in these events, particularly to the people who were living through them. Joseph probably did not sit rejoicing at the bottom of the pit, delighted that God was sending him into Egypt to fulfill His prophecy to Abraham; it is much more likely that he was overcome with grief and fear, wondering what was going to happen next—wondering, indeed, if he would be murdered by his own brothers. Yet the sovereign Lord retained control over Joseph's life. He is completely sovereign over all things in *our lives* too, and He has promised that He will always be faithful to His children. "And we know that all things work together for good to those who love God, to those who are the called according to His purpose" (Romans 8:28).

We are still responsible for our own actions.

The other side to the previous principle is that God's sovereignty does not exonerate us from our own responsibility. Joseph's brothers were fully responsible before God for attempting to murder him and for selling him into slavery.

God's plans cannot be thwarted by the actions of human beings, or even by Satan himself. So the Lord can and does use the wicked actions of evil men to accomplish His holy purposes. However, this is to the glory of God, not to the praise of wicked men. Joseph's brothers still had to answer for their deeds, even though God used those deeds to further His plans for Israel.

The good news is that the Lord also uses our obedience to further His purposes and bring glory to His name—and we grow in Christlikeness in the process. Joseph's responses to his brothers' deeds demonstrated this, and his life became a picture of the life of Christ.

Hatred and resentment lead to murder.

Cain demonstrated this principle when he became resentful of his brother's favor with the Lord (Genesis 4), finally taking it out in violence. Jacob's sons repeated this sin when they allowed their resentment to grow into hatred for Joseph. We run the same risk when we allow bitterness and resentment to grow toward others around us. We may never commit actual physical murder, but our very resentment and hatred are equivalent: "Whoever hates his brother is a murderer, and you know that no murderer has eternal life abiding in him" (1 John 3:15). "If someone says, 'I love God,' and hates his brother, he is a liar; for he who does not love his brother whom he has seen, how can he love God whom he has not seen?" (1 John 4:20)

When we find resentment growing toward another person, we must recognize that it is ultimately directed against God—as was the case with Cain. It is vital that we repent of these attitudes and submit ourselves to God's sovereignty, even when circumstances may seem unjust.

5. If there had been no hatred among the twelve sons, how might they have reacted differently to Joseph's dreams?

6. God wanted Joseph to go into Egypt for His own purposes. How do we balance the sovereignty of God with the sinful deeds of people?

7. Why did the brothers resent Joseph's dreams? What does this reveal about the deeper levels of their anger and resentment?

8. Why did God allow Joseph to suffer this mistreatment, when he had done nothing to deserve it? What does this teach about God's sovereignty?

9. Are you struggling with resentment or anger toward another person? What will you do this week to forgive that person?

10. What situations are you facing that seem out of control? How might the Lord be using those situations for His own purposes?

2

THE DAUGHTER OF JACOB

↳ HISTORICAL BACKGROUND ↲

We will now go backward in time a little from Study 1 and look at some events that transpired prior to Joseph being sold into slavery. Jacob and his family had been living in Shechem (north of Bethel; see the map in the Introduction) for several years, and he had purchased a parcel of land to live on. This was the first time that a descendant of Abraham had purchased land in Canaan, as far as we are told in Genesis, and it suggests that Jacob was settling down in Canaan.

This decision seems sensible from a purely logistical standpoint: Jacob had twelve sons, and most of them had families of their own. The people of Israel were becoming too numerous to wander about the land of Canaan as Abraham had done—at least, from man's perspective. But it was not God's plan that His people settle permanently in Canaan just yet. He had told Abraham that his descendants would "be strangers in a land that is not theirs," and that they would work as slaves for four hundred years before settling the land of Canaan (15:13–14). Until that time, He ordained that the children of Israel should live as pilgrims in the land that was their promised inheritance.

We met Jacob's twelve sons in Study 1, but now we will look at his daughter, Dinah. Dinah was born through Leah, as were six of the sons: Reuben, Simon, Levi, Judah, Issachar, and Zebulun. Dinah was the youngest of Leah's children, and she was probably between fourteen and sixteen years old at the time that our passage opens.

In Jacob's day, it would have been unusual for a teenage girl to go wandering alone about the streets of a strange city, yet this evidently is precisely what Dinah is about to do. We are not told the reasons for her excursion, but the results are quite dramatic.

⌁ READING GENESIS 34:1–31 ⌁

DINAH GOES OUT: *Jacob's family had purchased land in Shechem and settled there. One day, Dinah decided to go exploring on her own.*

1. DINAH: Dinah was the youngest, born to Leah after her sixth son, Zebulun (Genesis 30:20–21).

WENT OUT TO SEE THE DAUGHTERS OF THE LAND: The meaning of this phrase is uncertain. Josephus, the Jewish historian, claimed that this occurred during a Canaanite festival, and that Dinah went to see the women's finery. But her innocent and normal teenage curiosity led to great tragedy. Apparently she went by herself, which would have been unusual in that culture—ordinarily she would have been accompanied at least by her mother and female servants, and most likely also by her brothers. It is quite possible, then, that Dinah sneaked away without her father's consent.

2. SHECHEM: Jacob and his family were living in Shechem, which evidently was also a family name within the tribe of Canaanites who lived there. Places frequently took their names from the tribe or leader who settled there. In this case, Shechem was the son of the region's ruler. Jacob had purchased a piece of land from Shechem (33:19), which suggests that he was planning on settling there. This was not God's plan, however, and Jacob's decision to settle in with the Canaanites led to evil consequences.

TRAGEDY STRIKES: *Young Dinah was not protected by her brothers, who were tending their flocks in the fields. A wealthy young ruler took advantage of that.*

SAW HER . . . TOOK HER . . . LAY WITH HER . . . VIOLATED HER: This is a profound picture of the cycle of sin: Shechem indulged the desire of his eyes; then he reached out and took what he lusted after (as Eve did in Genesis 3); then he committed sin; and that sin brought forth death, as it always does: "Each one is tempted when he is drawn away by his own desires and enticed. Then, when desire has conceived, it gives birth to sin; and sin, when it is full-grown, brings forth death" (James 1:14–15).

3. STRONGLY ATTRACTED: This phrase is a single Hebrew word meaning "to cling to" or "to be joined with." It is the same word translated "joined" in Genesis 2:24: "Therefore a man shall leave his father and mother and be joined to his wife, and they shall become one flesh." Despite the violence of Shechem's crime, he joined his soul together with Dinah's.

HE LOVED THE YOUNG WOMAN: Shechem's sin was not undone or made right by his subsequent love toward Dinah. The same is true today. Neither is sin atoned for by our regrets, nor even by our attempts to "make it up" to someone we have injured.

4. GET ME THIS YOUNG WOMAN AS A WIFE: This is actually quite close to God's law given through Moses: "If a man finds a young woman who is a virgin, who is not betrothed, and he seizes her and lies with her, and they are found out, then the man who lay with her shall give to the young woman's father fifty shekels of silver, and she shall be his wife because he has humbled her; he shall not be permitted to divorce her all his days" (Deuteronomy 22:28–29).

5. HE HAD DEFILED DINAH: The word *defile* means to soil or pollute; to corrupt morally; to make unfit for holy purposes. This is a very serious concept, and it underscores the importance of sexual purity in God's people. Shechem had stolen something very precious from Dinah, and he had corrupted her in the process.

JACOB HELD HIS PEACE UNTIL THEY CAME: Some have suggested that Jacob was looking to his sons for guidance in this matter, but his reticence here may simply have been the course of wisdom, seeking counsel and taking his time before reacting. Still, Jacob himself should have exerted a strong, godly leadership in this situation. Yet his sons' subsequent actions suggest that he was not a strong leader in his own household.

7. THE SONS OF JACOB CAME IN FROM THE FIELD WHEN THEY HEARD IT: The brothers' initial response to this crime was proper: they dropped what they were doing and rushed to help. God's people today should be equally quick to draw together when a brother or sister is in difficulties.

HE HAD DONE A DISGRACEFUL THING: Sexual immorality has become so common in our culture that Christians are prone to turn a blind eye to it. But this is not the way God sees promiscuity; in His eyes, sexual intercourse outside the bounds of marriage is a grave wickedness. It is a disgraceful thing when God's people fail to keep themselves sexually pure—it is "a thing which ought not to be done" (v. 7).

SHECHEM REPENTS: *The young prince had committed a terrible crime against Dinah, but he quickly repented and tried to make restitution.*

8. GIVE HER TO HIM AS A WIFE: On the surface, this was a reasonable request, and it was in keeping with God's law. Dinah's honor had been violated, and it would be difficult for her to find a husband in the future because of Shechem's actions. The problem, however, was that the Canaanites did not serve God, and the people of Israel were not to intermarry with the world around them. It is understandable that Jacob was hesitant to make a decision here, because he was in a difficult position.

9. MAKE MARRIAGES WITH US: Abraham and Isaac had charged their sons not to take wives from among the Canaanites (Genesis 24; 28:1), and Jacob understood this principle. God's people are not to intermarry with those who do not serve Him, because it is similar to yoking together an ox and a donkey: the two animals are completely different and will attempt to plow in different directions. "Do not be unequally yoked together with unbelievers. For what fellowship has righteousness with lawlessness? And what communion has light with darkness?" (2 Corinthians 6:14)

10. THE LAND SHALL BE BEFORE YOU: Hamor's offer was perfectly legitimate, even generous: "Settle with us; trade with us; become one of us; own land and homes." But the Lord had already promised the land to Abraham's descendants, so from God's perspective, it wasn't Hamor's to give; the land was as good as Jacob's already. The Lord intended that His people live as pilgrims and strangers in the land during Jacob's day (Hebrews 11:9–10), so it was not time yet for the nation of Israel to settle into Canaan.

11. LET ME FIND FAVOR IN YOUR EYES: Shechem was asking for forgiveness, and he made it clear that he was willing to make whatever restitution for his crime that Dinah's family demanded. His crime was grievous, but his sorrow seems genuine. Shechem's behavior here was honorable.

THE BROTHERS CONSPIRE: *Jacob's sons were unwilling to accept Shechem's offer of restitution. Instead, they conspired to get revenge.*

13. THE SONS OF JACOB . . . SPOKE DECEITFULLY: Like father, like sons: Jacob's life had been characterized by deceit and craftiness, and his sons followed in his footsteps.

BECAUSE HE HAD DEFILED DINAH THEIR SISTER: There is no question that Shechem's violence toward Dinah was wicked, but all sin is wicked in the eyes of God. The young man had repented of his sin, and desired to make whatever restitution was called for—but the brothers responded with wickedness of their own.

14. WE CANNOT . . . GIVE OUR SISTER TO ONE WHO IS UNCIRCUMCISED: This was actually true, as the Lord did not want His people to intermarry with the Canaanites. But the Mosaic law (which had not yet been given) made provisions for Gentiles to be circumcised and to sojourn with God's people. The Lord's reason for selecting a chosen people in the first place was to make His grace evident to the entire world—not to simply bless the descendants of Abraham. Jacob's sons were grossly misusing God's provisions of grace to serve their own ends of revenge. "My beloved brethren, let every man be . . . slow to wrath; for the wrath of man does not produce the righteousness of God" (James 1:19–20).

THAT WOULD BE A REPROACH TO US: Ironically, what the sons of Jacob were about to do would also be a great reproach to them.

15. IF YOU WILL BECOME AS WE ARE . . . : Here again we find an ironic statement, since Shechem was the one who was being honorable in this conversation, while the sons of Jacob were being dishonorable.

16. . . . WE WILL BECOME ONE PEOPLE: This was an outright lie. Listen to what Paul wrote on this topic: "Therefore, putting away lying, 'Let each one of you speak truth with his neighbor,' for we are members of one another" (Ephesians 4:25).

19. THE YOUNG MAN DID NOT DELAY: This proved that Shechem's words were genuine, as he did not delay to do what Dinah's family required in making amends for his sin.

HE WAS MORE HONORABLE THAN ALL THE HOUSEHOLD OF HIS FATHER: This can be taken two ways. It indicates that Shechem was held in high esteem by his country-men, as demonstrated by the fact that the men of the city submitted themselves to the very painful and debilitating rite of circumcision. It also means that Shechem's actions, at least in part, were motivated by a genuine sorrow, while the actions of his father's house-hold apparently were motivated purely by a desire for financial gain.

23. WILL NOT THEIR . . . PROPERTY . . . BE OURS? : This seems to suggest that Hamor and Shechem were at least slightly motivated by the prospect of financial gain.

OVERKILL: *Jacob's sons take matters into their own hands, and go far beyond justice in carrying out their vengeance.*

24. EVERY MALE WAS CIRCUMCISED: God made the covenant of circumcision with Abraham (17:9–13) as an outward sign that the household and descendants of Abra-ham had cut off the flesh and entered into a new relationship of peace with God. The rite was to be carried out when a boy was only eight days old, although it also permit-ted circumcision of adult men. Circumcision of an adult, however, was very painful and incapacitating—as Jacob's sons were well aware. They were not interested in seeing the Canaanites make a covenant of peace with God; they were concerned with satisfying their own lust for revenge.

25. SIMEON AND LEVI: Dinah was born to Leah, as were Simeon and Levi. We saw in Study 1 that Jacob's firstborn son, Reuben, committed a gross sin that made him unfit to receive the birthright of the firstborn. Simeon and Levi were the second and third sons of Jacob, respectively, but this sin may be part of the reason they, too, did not receive the birthright. We will see in a later study that the birthright was eventually passed on to Judah, who was fourth in line. Jesus was born through the line of Judah—not through Reuben, Simeon, or Levi.

26. THEY KILLED HAMOR AND SHECHEM: The punishment required by Mosaic law for Shechem's crime was to make restitution and to marry the violated woman—not the death penalty, and most certainly not the death of the young man's family as well. But Jacob's sons went beyond even that extremity and slaughtered all the men of the city. This was nothing but the indulgence of bloodlust, and there was no justice in it.

27. THE SONS OF JACOB: Simeon and Levi were guilty of murder, but all the sons apparently took a share in the guilt by plundering the dead. This sad perversion of family unity would repeat itself when the brothers united together to murder Joseph. (This event in Dinah's life took place prior to the passages in Study 1.)

30. THEY WILL GATHER THEMSELVES TOGETHER AGAINST ME AND KILL ME: Jacob's primary concern was his own safety, not the people who were slain or the wicked behavior of his sons. The sad irony of this is that Jacob would not have been faced with this danger if he had not tried to settle in Shechem in the first place.

31. SHOULD HE TREAT OUR SISTER LIKE A HARLOT?: Yet Shechem had *not* treated Dinah like a harlot in the long run. The sons of Jacob were trying to justify their own wickedness, but Shechem's honorable attempts at restitution point accusingly at their guilt.

ᨳ First Impressions ᨳ

1. *What motivated Dinah to go into town on her own? Do you think her actions were justified, or unwise?*

2. *What motivated Dinah's brothers to carry out such a bloody revenge? If you had been in their place, what would you have done?*

3. *Do you think Shechem's sorrow was genuine or insincere? Was his offer of marriage a sufficient recompense for what he had done? Support your answers from this passage.*

4. *If you had been in Jacob's place, how would you have responded to Shechem's repentance?*

↳ Some Key Principles ↰

God's people must live as pilgrims and strangers in this world.

God had promised Abraham that his descendants would inherit the entire land of Canaan, but he himself was called to live like a nomad, moving from place to place without ever inheriting a single acre. The New Testament uses his example to teach us that Christians will inherit the eternal kingdom of God—but that kingdom is not of this world, and we must not lose sight of that fact.

Abraham "waited for the city which has foundations, whose builder and maker is God" (Hebrews 11:10), and his expectations were never realized in his lifetime. The same is true for God's people today: our true home is eternal, and the things of this world that consume our time and energies can distract us from storing up eternal treasures. Jacob lost sight of this when he bought land in Shechem and began to settle down.

It is not wrong to have a home and a career and to "put down roots" in a community. The danger lies in forgetting that these things are only temporary. Our focus must always be on investing into the kingdom of God, investing for eternity rather than for today.

God hates sin, but He also forgives sin.

Shechem was a lustful young man, and he lacked the discipline to control his passions. He saw a beautiful young girl, allowed his lust to control him, and ended by defiling her. His sin brought shame both upon himself and upon an innocent girl—but then he repented of that sin and sought to make restitution.

In God's eyes, all sins are an absolute affront to his holy character—every act of disobedience, no matter how small and insignificant in our eyes, brings defilement and reproach upon us and upon others. But God, unlike Jacob's sons, also makes provision for repentance and restitution. What's more, He also provides His Holy Spirit to believers in Jesus Christ, and the Spirit's role in part is to convict us of sin and urge us toward repentance.

Every one of us is guilty of wickedness, just as Shechem and Jacob's sons were guilty before God:"If we say that we have no sin, we deceive ourselves, and the truth is not in us" (1 John 1:8). But every one of us also has the opportunity to repent of sins and to be fully restored to an unbroken relationship with our Creator:"If we confess our sins, He is faithful and just to forgive us our sins and to cleanse us from all unrighteousness" (1 John 1:9).

Vengeance belongs to God, not to us.

Shechem's sin against Dinah brought disgrace upon her entire family, and her brothers were right to be angry. They were wrong, however, to take their own revenge upon the people of that city; in so doing, they were as guilty as Shechem for not controlling their own passions.

We all suffer at the hands of other people from time to time, and sometimes we can be called to suffer greatly. However, we must remember to view such sufferings as God's tools of purification and strengthening for us. Those who hate us are not permitted to cause evil in our lives unless God allows it—and when He allows it, He does so for a reason.

God's reasons for allowing His children to suffer are always intended to bring glory to His name. It may be that He is working to bring the wrongdoer to salvation, or perhaps He is working on making us more like Christ. Whether we can see a reason or not, we must never repay evil with evil. "Beloved, do not avenge yourselves, but rather give place to wrath; for it is written,'Vengeance is Mine, I will repay,' says the Lord. Therefore 'If your enemy is hungry, feed him; if he is thirsty, give him a drink; for in so doing you will heap coals of fire on his head.' Do not be overcome by evil, but overcome evil with good" (Romans 12:19–21).

God calls His people to be instruments of grace, not weapons of wrath.

The Lord had instituted the covenant of circumcision with Abraham's descendants in order to provide an outward, visible sign to the world that the Israelites were His people. That covenant was for God's glory, not because Israel had done something to earn His favor. Jacob's sons, however, used God's provision of grace for their own lustful purposes, and in so doing they brought disgrace on God's name.

↫ DIGGING DEEPER ↬

5. What motivated Jacob, in your opinion, to purchase land near Shechem? Was this wise or unwise?

6. Have you ever known someone who committed a grievous sin, but then later repented? What fruits of repentance (evidence of a changed heart) did that person exhibit in his or her life?

7. How should Jacob have responded to Shechem's sin? Did Jacob do the right thing regarding Shechem? Regarding his sons?

8. When have you seen God's grace demonstrated by someone who was wronged? Is there a circumstance in your life right now in which you can demonstrate grace toward someone else?

9. *How do you respond when someone wrongs you? Do you take revenge, or offer forgiveness?*

10. *How do you respond when you have committed a sin against someone else? Do you seek forgiveness and offer restitution?*

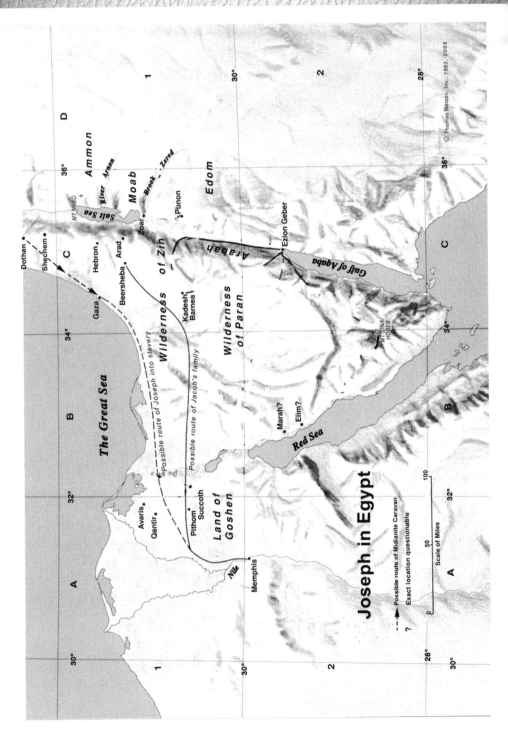

Joseph in Egypt

Possible route of Midianite Caravan

? Exact location questionable

Scale of Miles

0   50   100

Possible route of Joseph into slavery

Possible route of Jacob's family

The Great Sea

Land of Goshen

Wilderness of Zin

Wilderness of Paran

Red Sea

Gulf of Aqaba

Arabah

Ammon

Moab

Edom

Salt Sea

MT. NEBO

River Arnon

Brook Zered

Dothan

Shechem

Gaza

Beersheba

Hebron

Arad

Kadesh Barnea

Zoar

Punon

Ezion Geber

MT. SINAI HOREB

Marah?

Elim?

Avaris

Qantir

Pithom

Succoth

Memphis

Nile

© Thomas Nelson, Inc. 1983, 2008

— 3 —
JOSEPH THE SLAVE

⤳ HISTORICAL BACKGROUND ⤴

Let us now return to our consideration of Joseph, who has been sold into slavery by his brothers. A caravan of Midianites bought him and took him into Egypt at age seventeen. We do not know what occurred along the way on that trip, nor what it was like to be bought and sold at a slave market in Egypt—but we can safely assume that none of it was pleasant.

Joseph eventually was purchased by a man named Potiphar, who held an important role in Pharaoh's kingdom as the captain of the guard. It is not known exactly what this role entailed, but it seems likely that it included oversight of Egypt's prisons. Potiphar was a wealthy and influential man, and it would be profitable for a lowly slave to find favor with him.

In Joseph's day, Egypt was the most influential world power, a place of great luxury and technology. Its culture and religious beliefs influenced all of Canaan and beyond, and its military was unsurpassed. By contrast, Jacob's family had been nomadic shepherds, roaming from place to place throughout Canaan for several generations. They lived in tents, while the Egyptians lived in permanent houses—and Egyptian architecture was grand even by modern standards.

Joseph was entering a nation that spoke a different language, operated under different cultural norms, and served foreign gods. To make matters worse, the Egyptians detested shepherds and considered such people unfit to eat with. They also bought and sold slaves, a social class that is at the bottom of any societal hierarchy. With his language and cultural differences, religious animosities, social background, and lack of status as a slave, Joseph was about as low in Egyptian society as any human could sink.

Add to all of this the fact that he had been betrayed by his own brothers, and one can get a sense of the utter despair and heartbreak Joseph must have suffered. Most of us would have become bitter and angry in such a situation, and we might have made every attempt to escape, motivated by a sincere desire for revenge—and these reactions might be understandable from a human perspective.

Furthermore, as we read about Joseph's enslavement, we will see how the "wheel of fortune" swung him violently from his position of favor at the top of the wheel to the very bottom—and then back up again—only to be dashed down once more. These dizzying swings of fortune would challenge anyone's faith, and most of us would respond with anger or despair. Yet Joseph's response was worlds apart—in fact, his response was not of this world at all, but was, instead, focused on eternity.

⤳ READING GENESIS 39:1–23 ⤳

SOLD INTO EGYPT: *Jacob's brothers have betrayed him—initially intending to murder him outright, finally settling on simply selling him as a slave.*

1. TAKEN DOWN TO EGYPT: Joseph's brothers had sold him as a slave to a camel caravan of traders (Genesis 37). The map on page 26 shows the probable route that the caravan followed. The distance was more than two hundred miles, and the journey probably took a week or two.

POTIPHAR: This name may have been a title for his position, just as "Pharaoh" was a title rather than a personal name.

OFFICER OF PHARAOH, CAPTAIN OF THE GUARD, AN EGYPTIAN: This lengthy description underscores the immense gulf that would have existed between Joseph and his new master. Potiphar was an Egyptian, and Egyptians despised shepherds in general and Hebrews in particular. He was the captain of the guard, which meant that he had a military background and was probably cultured and well educated—in contrast to Joseph's rural, domestic upbringing. He was also a member of Pharaoh's retinue, quite possibly the chief of Pharaoh's personal bodyguard, which meant that he was probably of noble birth and royal connections. From a human perspective, there is little chance that such a man would pay any attention to a slave like Joseph.

2. THE LORD WAS WITH JOSEPH: It is easy for modern readers to gloss over this important fact, but if we put ourselves in Joseph's place, it is quite a startling statement. Joseph had gone out to the pastures to visit his brothers on his father's errand, not expecting anything unusual. But his brothers had seen him coming and plotted to murder him. They had thrown him into a pit, then sold him into slavery. He had been carried against his will, far from home into a hostile foreign culture, and was living as a despised slave. It would be hard in those circumstances to believe that the Lord was with you—yet Joseph clung firmly to that conviction, and the Lord blessed him greatly.

HE WAS A SUCCESSFUL MAN: This is one way in which the Lord blessed Joseph, bringing him success in all his endeavors. Potiphar evidently noticed that Joseph excelled in whatever tasks he was given, and that probably led to Joseph's quick advancement.

HE WAS IN THE HOUSE OF HIS MASTER: This indicates that Joseph had found favor in the eyes of Potiphar and was entrusted with household duties as opposed to the more rigorous field work. It also shows that Potiphar did not expect Joseph to run away, and that he trusted him even further with access to his own home. Jewish tradition holds that Joseph was in Potiphar's household for a full year—a very short time for one of his lowly stature to rise to a position of such trust.

3. HIS MASTER SAW THAT THE LORD WAS WITH HIM: This simple statement encapsulates the very reason that God chose the descendants of Abraham in the first place, as it was His plan to show forth His grace and character to all people. By observing the life of a faithful servant of God, the people of all nations could learn more about the character of God.

4. OVERSEER OF HIS HOUSE: This is a remarkable change of fortunes for Joseph. Within a short period of time, he had risen from the lowliest of slaves to second in command of Potiphar's household—and Potiphar himself was a man of distinction in Egypt. If the story ended here, it would still be a testament to the faithfulness of God toward those who follow Him. But this level of authority was not the end of God's plan; He had given Joseph prophetic dreams that still needed to be fulfilled (Genesis 37:5–10).

5. THE LORD BLESSED THE EGYPTIAN'S HOUSE FOR JOSEPH'S SAKE: Here is a fulfillment of one of God's promises to Abraham: "I will bless those who bless you, and I will curse him who curses you; and in you all the families of the earth shall be blessed" (Genesis 12:3).

6. HE LEFT ALL THAT HE HAD IN JOSEPH'S HAND: Joseph may have felt at this point that things had turned out rather well, despite his previous sufferings. He might have become content to remain in that situation indefinitely—after all, it was (in worldly terms) an infinite improvement over his nomadic shepherd's life. But this was not what the Lord had planned for him, and his fortunes were about to change for the worse once again.

POTIPHAR'S WIFE: *Joseph had risen to a position of honor that would be enough for any career—but his master's wife had some ideas of her own.*

JOSEPH WAS HANDSOME: He was eighteen or nineteen by this time and had grown into a strong, well-built young man. He appeared to those around him to be very gifted, as he succeeded in everything that he put his hand to, and he was very good-looking besides. Joseph was a man who turned heads.

7. LONGING EYES: The Hebrew for this phrase could be transliterated as "swept away by her eyes." Potiphar's wife was swept off her feet, carried away with her desire for this virile young man.

LIE WITH ME: Potiphar was probably very busy with his duties, and the fact that he had no knowledge of his household affairs indicates that he may have been absent much of the time. Some scholars have even suggested that he may have been a eunuch, although the text makes no such mention. Whatever the circumstances, it would have been easy for Joseph to rationalize yielding to the demands of Potiphar's wife.

8. BUT HE REFUSED: Joseph was in the prime of his manhood, subject to the temptations of the flesh that are common to all people. He was also cut off from his family and loved ones, a stranger in a strange land, and quite likely felt great loneliness. Yet he demonstrated a steely determination to remain pure, even at the cost of denying strong fleshly desires.

9. . . . AND SIN AGAINST GOD: Here is the foundation of Joseph's determination: he recognized that he was directly accountable to God for his actions. He did not say, "How can I sin against Potiphar?" He recognized that all sin is ultimately committed against God Himself, and this perspective helped him remain strong. David recognized this as well, when he committed adultery with Bathsheba: "Against You, You only, have I sinned," he said, "and done this evil in Your sight" (Psalm 51:4).

10. SHE SPOKE TO JOSEPH DAY BY DAY: It is difficult enough to resist powerful temptation once, but having it repeated day after day can seem intolerable. Yet God does not ever permit us to be tempted beyond the point of endurance: "No temptation has overtaken you except such as is common to man; but God is faithful, who will not allow you to be tempted beyond what you are able, but with the temptation will also make the way of escape, that you may be able to bear it" (1 Corinthians 10:13).

HE DID NOT HEED HER: Joseph went beyond the point of repeatedly refusing her advances; he refused even to discuss it with her. Such a debate would only have increased his tempter's opportunities. It always does. In fact, this is exactly where Eve fell into trouble, as she held a debate with the serpent (Genesis 3).

OR TO BE WITH HER: And to his refusal to discuss the issue, Joseph added the refusal even to be in her company. Again, Eve should have fled the very presence of the serpent, once it became plain that he was urging her to disobey God's command. If we follow Joseph's example, we will avoid the very company of anyone who suggests that we disregard God's Word.

FALSELY ACCUSED: *Potiphar's wife is forced to recognize that Joseph will not yield to her sinful demands—and she responds with venom.*

11. JOSEPH WENT INTO THE HOUSE TO DO HIS WORK: Yet, in the midst of this terrific persecution, Joseph still remained faithful to his duties. This is another aspect of his faithfulness to God: he steadfastly refused to sin against God, while also steadfastly remaining faithful to what God had given him to do. It is important to realize, however, that even our complete faithfulness will not protect us from facing temptation. The Lord does permit temptation to enter our lives for the purpose of making us more like Christ, and the temptation itself is not sin.

12. HE LEFT HIS GARMENT IN HER HAND, AND FLED AND RAN OUTSIDE: "If your eye causes you to sin," Jesus said, "pluck it out. It is better for you to enter the kingdom of God with one eye, rather than having two eyes, to be cast into hell fire" (Mark 9:47). Later, the apostle Paul wrote, "Flee also youthful lusts" (2 Timothy 2:22). Thousands of years in advance of the admonitions of Paul and Christ, Joseph was already responding in Christlike fashion to the persistent woman's advances.

13. WHEN SHE SAW THAT HE HAD LEFT HIS GARMENT IN HER HAND: Our faithfulness to God will become evident to those around us. Even Potiphar's wife eventually was forced to recognize that Joseph was not going to yield to her temptations. There are times when such steadfast faithfulness will cause the world to hate us, as was the case with Joseph.

14. TO MOCK US: Those who are committed to the world's system will resent the people of God. When we speak out against the world's wickedness, we will face the hatred of many, and their response will be to accuse us of being "judgmental" and "self-righteous." Even Lot found this to be true when he urged the men of Sodom not to attack the Lord's angels: "Then they said, 'This one came in to stay here, and he keeps acting as a judge; now we will deal worse with you than with them.' So they pressed hard against the man Lot, and came near to break down the door" (Genesis 19:9).

16. SHE KEPT HIS GARMENT WITH HER: From a human perspective, Joseph did not stand a chance against this false accusation. He had risen to authority in Potiphar's home, yet he was still a slave—and a Hebrew slave, at that. It was his word against the word of his master's wife, and the outcome seemed clear from the beginning. Yet this does not account for the sovereignty of God, and the outcome of the situation was entirely in His hands, no matter what the odds were against Joseph.

SENT OFF TO PRISON: *Joseph has gone from home life to slavery to authority—and now back to slavery again, as he makes another new start in prison.*

20. PUT HIM INTO THE PRISON: It is quite possible that Potiphar was in charge over this prison, although he probably was not the warden. Once again, Joseph's fortunes changed suddenly and dramatically; and once again, he lost everything in one sudden stroke—even though he was completely innocent.

21. BUT THE LORD WAS WITH JOSEPH: Once again, if we put ourselves in Joseph's place, we can see how hard it must have been to maintain this perspective. It would be all too easy to fall into despair, believing that the Lord had abandoned us or proven unfaithful. But Joseph clung to his conviction that the Lord is faithful, and will never abandon His children. And his faith in God was well placed. Listen to the words of the Lord from the book of Isaiah: "But Zion said, 'The LORD has forsaken me, and my Lord has forgotten me.' Can a woman forget her nursing child, and not have compassion on the son of her womb? Surely they may forget, yet I will not forget you. See, I have inscribed you on the palms of My hands; your walls are continually before Me'" (49:14–16).

22. ALL THE PRISONERS WHO WERE IN THE PRISON: This would prove very important in Joseph's future, another proof that God was in complete control over all of his circumstances.

23. WHATEVER HE DID, THE LORD MADE IT PROSPER: Once again, the Lord blessed Joseph's faithfulness, and that blessing became evident to the people around him. Wherever he went, whether slave or free, Joseph was a blessing to those around him. This is what it means to be one of God's children.

∽ FIRST IMPRESSIONS ∽

1. *Put yourself in Joseph's place. How would you have reacted to find yourself in a slave caravan, heading toward Egypt? How would you have responded to your new masters?*

2. What evidences are there in this passage of God's control over Joseph's circumstances? How much of God's control would Joseph have seen at the time?

3. In what ways was Joseph faithful to the Lord during his time in Potiphar's house?

4. Why did Joseph rise so quickly to a position of authority? What part did God play in that? What part did he play?

ᔗ Some Key Principles ᔗ

God is in control of every event in our lives—both good and bad.

It is startling to consider the dramatic rises and falls in Joseph's fortunes—and the story isn't even finished yet. It is easy for us to read his history and see the hand of God at work in his life; but it was not so easy for Joseph when he was living through these events. It would have been much easier to yield to despair or bitterness.

But God had absolute control over all these events, and He was not haphazard in the things that He allowed Joseph to go through. During his tenure in Potiphar's household, for example, Joseph learned important managerial skills that he would need later in life. God sees far beyond the immediate horizon of our daily lives, and His plan is perfect. He knows exactly what each of His children needs to learn, what qualities we need to develop in fulfilling that plan.

When we undergo deep suffering or elevated success, it is easy to lose sight of this important principle. The Lord is in control of everything that touches our lives— including the mundane, daily grind of ordinary life, which itself can be the most valuable training in the long run. We make the most of His character development when we keep this truth in mind.

Do not try to simply endure strong temptation—run away!

There is much that goes unstated in this passage; the Scriptures do not tell us what powerful emotions Joseph was experiencing as a slave in Egypt. He was a healthy young man in his prime, cut off from family and friends, lonely in a foreign land, and the temptations of Potiphar's wife must have been powerful indeed. But Joseph demonstrated the correct way to deal with such temptations: he fled! He refused to discuss the subject with the one who tempted him, declined even to be in her company. He evidently made a point of trying never to be alone in the house with her, and on the last occasion did so inadvertently. When he found himself in that dangerous predicament, he ran away quite literally, even to the point of leaving his cloak in her hands.

Some situations require us to persevere in daily decisions to please our Father, while others can only be overcome by running away. But whatever your situation, "be sober, be vigilant; because your adversary the devil walks about like a roaring lion, seeking whom he may devour. Resist him," wrote Peter, "steadfast in the faith, knowing that the same sufferings are experienced by your brotherhood in the world" (1 Peter 5:8–9). Sometimes, the best way to resist a roaring lion is to flee.

The Lord blesses us when we are obedient.

It almost seems incongruous to read that the Lord was blessing Joseph by sending him into Egypt as a slave, but God's purposes go far beyond the immediate moment. The Lord had placed Joseph in a situation over which he had no control, but there was one thing that he *could* control: his responses to that situation.

Joseph focused on doing the things that he was given to do—which meant obeying his slave master and doing his work carefully and earnestly. There are times when our greatest act of obedience to the Lord is simply to submit humbly to the circumstances that are beyond our control. Our submission to His will allows our Father to pour out His fullest blessings into our lives. "Whatever your hand finds to do, do it with your might" (Ecclesiastes 9:10). In the long run, our Father will bless that attitude.

Our faithfulness and obedience will be a strong testimony to the world around us.

Potiphar's entire household could see that God was with Joseph because of the young man's attitude and obedience. Joseph may not have realized that he was being watched so closely, but the world will always pay attention to a Christian's life to see whether the teachings of Jesus are true. It is important to understand that this was the very reason that God selected a "chosen people" in the first place: to show forth His love and goodness to the world, and to bring salvation to sinners through the Messiah. The same holds true for Christians today: the Lord allows us to remain in the world in order to show forth His salvation plan to those who do not know Him.

As we quietly and faithfully obey His Word, people will be watching. Our faith in His promises will be a strong testimony to the truth of those promises. God's faithfulness to bless and care for His children will be visible to those around us—and these things will be our most powerful witness in the world.

↳ Digging Deeper ↲

5. *What excuses might Joseph have made for giving in to Potiphar's wife?*

6. *How did Joseph overcome the temptations of Potiphar's wife? What was his focus during that struggle?*

7. What aspects of Joseph's situation were beyond his power to change? What aspects were within his control?

8. When have you seen the Lord bring great blessing out of sorrow in your own life or the life of someone you know?

↳ TAKING IT PERSONALLY ↶

9. What situations in your life are beyond your power to change? How would the Lord have you respond to those situations?

10. What people might be watching your life to see whether Christianity is true? Is your life providing a faithful witness to the truth of the gospel?

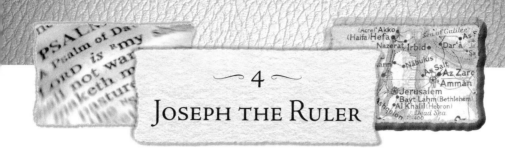

～ 4 ～
JOSEPH THE RULER

～ HISTORICAL BACKGROUND ～

During his imprisonment, Joseph met an important member of Pharaoh's household and interpreted his dream accurately. (We'll cover this story more in a later study.) Later, Pharaoh also had a dream, a very strange one, which none of his wise men could interpret. Suddenly, Joseph's name was remembered, and Pharaoh sent for him out of the prison. It is here that this study will begin.

As before, the Lord gave Joseph the correct interpretation of a prophetic dream. Through it, God was warning Pharaoh that a terrible worldwide famine was coming. First, though, there would be seven years of plenty, with undreamed-of harvests and abundance. That time would be followed by seven years of drought that would eat up all the excess of the previous years of plenty. This drought would be so severe that it would threaten all peoples in the known world.

But God was not caught off guard by this development. He had been planning for this contingency all along, and had trained up a special man to lead the world through it. This man, of course, was Joseph, and in these passages we will see how his time as a slave in Potiphar's house was actually preparing him for this very job.

Leadership is not something to be undertaken lightly in any forum, as the Lord holds leaders to a high standard of accountability (Hebrews 13:17). Paul tells us in Romans 13 that God Himself chooses who will reign over us, even in the worldly political realm. We are called upon to obey those authorities, including paying taxes and observing the laws of the land. Complaining about high taxes is probably universal, yet in general we are not faced with the financial burden that threatened Egypt under Joseph's leadership.

In fact, Joseph endured a number of immensely threatening circumstances that would have toppled the authority of most governments. These included the complete collapse of the monetary system and a worldwide famine that endangered the lives of all people. He was forced to institute a hefty income tax, to take ownership of all private property, and to move large numbers of people away from their homes and into cities. Any of these circumstances have produced rebellion and even revolution in other nations at other times, but Joseph's leadership brought the people through without the loss of their devotion to Pharaoh.

In this study, we will examine Joseph's gifts as a leader during a time of great worldwide crisis, and we will see that God had planned for this all along, and had prepared His man for this very situation.

⤳ Reading Genesis 41:33–57 ⤳

Pharaoh's Dream: *Joseph has been in prison for several years when Pharaoh has a prophetic dream. None of his wise men can interpret it, so he calls upon Joseph.*

33. let Pharaoh select a discerning and wise man: Joseph had been released from prison in order to interpret a dream of Pharaoh's concerning the future. With precision, Joseph told him the meaning of his dream: there would be seven years of plenty, followed by seven years of devastating famine. (We will look back at what happened during Joseph's imprisonment in Study 8.) He suggested that Pharaoh choose a leader to oversee preparations for the coming crisis.

34. collect one-fifth of the produce of the land of Egypt: Joseph further outlined a wise plan for how to prepare for the coming famine: Take advantage of the coming seven years of plenty by taxing the nation at 20 percent of all crops. Set up storage centers around Egypt, and hold that food in reserve for the seven years of drought and famine that would follow.

37. the advice was good in the eyes of Pharaoh: Here we see two principles at work which we noticed in the last study: the blessing of God, and the preparation of Joseph. The Lord was still with Joseph, blessing the work of his hands—and, in this case, his interpretation of dreams and wisdom for the future. The Lord also had prepared Joseph for just this situation by giving him experience at managing the household affairs of Potiphar. If he had not been a slave in Potiphar's house, he might not have conceived this wise plan. But the Lord had prepared him for just this event, and as a result his advice was sound and wise.

38. a man in whom is the Spirit of God: Once again we discover that God's involvement in the life of Joseph was readily apparent to the people around him. Joseph had made himself available to God, accepting the circumstances that the Lord brought into his life, and as a result even Pharaoh could discern that the Spirit of the Lord was working in his life.

39. GOD HAS SHOWN YOU ALL THIS: What an amazing statement, spoken to a slave! Yet Joseph did not allow himself to become puffed up by the great things that God had done through him. We will see in Study 6 that Joseph gave all the glory to God.

JOSEPH IS ELEVATED: *Pharaoh recognizes that God is with Joseph and immediately places him in command over all Egypt.*

40. YOU SHALL BE OVER MY HOUSE: This is precisely the same arrangement that Joseph had in Potiphar's household—but on a much grander scale. He became the head over all of Egypt, the greatest nation on earth in his day, and ruled with absolute authority, subject only to Pharaoh himself. Yet the Lord had prepared him for this powerful position through the experiences he'd had as a slave in Potiphar's house. Had he not submitted to the Lord's training as a slave, he would not have been equipped for this tremendous responsibility.

42. SIGNET RING . . . FINE LINEN . . . GOLD CHAIN: These were symbols of royalty and authority. The signet ring gave Joseph the authority to make laws and proclamations throughout Egypt. The fine linen and gold chain indicated his status as a high-ranking member of Pharaoh's own household. There is also a wonderful example here of God's faithfulness. Joseph had been given a special robe by his father (37:3), indicating that his father held him in high esteem among his brothers—but his brothers had stripped him of this robe and sold him into slavery. Now, after many years of faithfulness through great suffering, Joseph had his robe returned—with interest. His new clothing represented an even higher degree of honor and esteem than what he had lost previously.

44. WITHOUT YOUR CONSENT NO MAN MAY LIFT HIS HAND OR FOOT: There is a wonderful divine justice in this decree. Joseph had humbly submitted himself to the violence of his brothers when they lifted their hands against him, and he had continued to submit himself under the hand of God's training. As a result, he was found fit to judge over the "lifting of hands" throughout the nation of Egypt.

45. PHARAOH CALLED JOSEPH'S NAME ZAPHNATH-PAANEAH: The meaning of this name is unclear, but it might mean "God speaks and He lives." It was common in the ancient world to give a person a new name when he became the subject of a foreign king. This was also the case with Daniel and his friends (Daniel 1:6–7). In the same way, the Lord will give each of His children new names in His eternal kingdom (Revelation 2:17), and Jesus Himself will bear a new name for all eternity: KING OF KINGS AND LORD OF LORDS (Revelation 19:16).

Joseph's Blessings: *The Lord now restores to Joseph far more than what he had lost when sold into slavery.*

46. Joseph was thirty years old: He was seventeen when he was sold into slavery, so he had endured thirteen years of captivity and enslavement.

49. until he stopped counting, for it was immeasurable: This is how the Lord blesses those who obey Him, pouring out blessings in immeasurable abundance. "'Try Me now in this,' Says the Lord of hosts, 'if I will not open for you the windows of heaven and pour out for you such blessing that there will not be room enough to receive it'" (Malachi 3:10).

51. Manasseh: meaning "causing to forget." The Lord blessed Joseph so abundantly that it was as if he had never suffered in the first place. Even his lost family had been restored to the extent that he forgot his grief.

52. Ephraim: meaning "double fruit." Like Joseph, Job had also suffered tremendously, but the Lord rewarded his faithfulness with double what he had lost (Job 42:10). Now he was rewarding Joseph the same way.

57. the famine was severe in all lands: Pharoah's dream prophesying a fourteen-year cycle of plenty and famine was fulfilled completely.

⌁ Reading Genesis 47:11–27 ⌁

Joseph Takes Command: *The seven years of plenty arrived, just as Joseph had said. During that time Joseph collected vast storehouses of food. But then came the seven years of famine . . .*

11. Joseph situated his father and his brothers: Time had passed, and Joseph had been fully reconciled with his brothers. His father Jacob has moved with his entire household into Egypt to escape the famine, and Joseph's skilled leadership found room for everyone.

in the best of the land: We saw in an earlier study how Jacob's habitual favoritism made trouble for his sons. But here we see the positive aspect of that trait in his son Joseph, who did not hesitate to save the best for his own family.

12. Joseph provided . . . bread: The entire known world of Joseph's day was suffering from a devastating drought and famine, and the only place that had sufficient food was Egypt. This provision was thanks to Joseph's diligent planning and leadership, and his leadership was skillful simply because he obeyed God. The leader who submits himself to God's Word will be blessed and will lead with skill.

14. Joseph brought the money into Pharaoh's house: One of the traits of Joseph's life was faithfulness: he remained faithful to his master—first in Potiphar's house, then as Pharaoh's trusted minister. This is another important aspect of leadership: a good leader will first be a good follower, faithful to his superiors.

Everything Collapses: *The people run out of food, the monetary systems collapse, and the whole world is in danger of starvation. Yet Joseph remains firm.*

15. the money failed: This famine was extreme, to the extent that it caused a collapse of Egypt's monetary system. Yet this extremity did not cause Joseph's leadership to collapse, as it has at other times and places in history. Joseph overcame the danger by instituting a bartering system.

17. he fed them with bread in exchange for all their livestock: This may sound extreme, but we must remember that the livestock would not have survived otherwise. If there was no food for the people, there was certainly none for the animals.

19. Buy us and our land: This famine led to the entire collapse of the governmental order in Joseph's time, yet Joseph remained steadfast through it all. Monarchs down through human history have been brought down during such tumultuous times, and nations have collapsed. But God was with Joseph throughout this dreadful ordeal, and the nation of Egypt—along with Pharaoh's throne—were kept intact because of Joseph's leadership, and his leadership was sound because he attended to God's Word.

20. the land became Pharaoh's: The system of government Joseph instituted resembled the feudal system in Europe during the Middle Ages.

21. he moved them into the cities: Here we find yet another major change that has caused changes in governmental authorities at other times, as Joseph changed the demographics of the entire nation of Egypt.

24. you shall give one-fifth to Pharaoh: This is the first mention of an income tax in Scripture. The Lord would later use a national income tax to send Joseph and Mary to Bethlehem, where His Son was to be born (Luke 2:1).

25. You have saved our lives: Throughout all these tumultuous changes, the people remained loyal to Joseph—and through him, to Pharaoh. This alone is a testimony to the strength of Joseph's leadership.

27. Israel dwelt in the land of Egypt: The Lord did these things to bless Joseph, but His purposes also went well beyond that. He had intended that Abraham's descendants should live in Egypt for four hundred years (15:13), and this was His way of moving Israel's entire family there. God's purposes in our personal lives include our own blessings, but His plans are always far bigger than we can see.

↳ First Impressions ↲

1. How do you think Joseph felt when he was whisked out of prison and made the ruler of all Egypt? How would you have reacted in that situation?

2. If you were in Joseph's place, what temptations might you face concerning those who had mistreated you in the past? How did Joseph treat those people?

3. How had God prepared Joseph to take command in Egypt? Give specific examples.

4. *If you had been an Egyptian landowner, how might you have reacted to Joseph's acts as your sovereign? How do you react to civic obligations in your own life?*

⌒ Some Key Principles ⌒

A godly leader is first a godly follower.

Joseph demonstrated this principle in his own life. God tested him when he was sold into slavery in Egypt, and Joseph remained faithful. The Lord gave him lowly jobs as a slave to Potiphar, and later as a falsely accused prisoner, and Joseph performed those jobs faithfully.

These roles as slave and prisoner were actually preparing Joseph for his role as a powerful leader, but he did not know that at the time. His focus was merely on obeying God and diligently performing whatever tasks he was given to do. He learned the lesson of obeying authority, whether that authority was a slave master or a prison guard.

The reason that submission is so important in a leader is that the godly leader will continue to be in submission, regardless of his or her position of authority—submission to the Word of God. Joseph demonstrated this, as well, believing the prophecy that the Lord had given through Pharaoh's dreams, and acting accordingly. In order to be a godly leader, a person must first learn to submit to the will of God.

The Lord appoints our leaders, even in the realm of worldly politics.

This principle can seem hard to accept at times, when a nation's leaders are ungodly and unjust. This was certainly the case in Israel under numerous wicked kings; Elijah suffered under the ungodly leadership of King Ahab and his notorious wife, Jezebel. Jesus Himself submitted to unwise authority when He was sent to the cross.

God's people are called to submit themselves to those in authority—in the home, at church, in the workplace, and in society as a whole. "Let every soul be subject to the governing authorities," wrote Paul. "For there is no authority except from God, and the authorities that exist are appointed by God. Therefore whoever resists the authority resists the ordinance of God, and those who resist will bring judgment on themselves" (Romans 13:1–2).

There may be times when the authority figures over us seem inept or unjust or even openly wicked, yet we must recognize that their authority comes from God, and we are placed under it for His purposes. There can be few situations more unjust than slavery, yet Joseph submitted—and God blessed his faithfulness.

The Lord uses trials to prepare us for greater tasks.

Joseph suffered greatly when his brothers betrayed him, and later when Potiphar's wife falsely accused him. But these trials were permitted by God, even though it might have been hard for Joseph to see God's hand at the time. The Lord was using those trials to strengthen Joseph's faith, and also to teach him very practical lessons that he would need later. Joseph had no idea that he would one day rule over all Egypt, and he consequently could not have prepared himself with the skills that would be required. Only the Lord knew those things, and He used disappointments and setbacks and slavery and imprisonment to train Joseph for the future.

We may not become world leaders, but the Lord's plans for our future are still important in the eternal scheme. And the day will come when all of His people shall rule the world—in fact, we will rule with Him over all creation, for all eternity. He is preparing each of us now to be ready for that great role of leadership, and He uses every circumstance in our lives for our spiritual good—including suffering and hardship (see Romans 8:28).

✌ DIGGING DEEPER ↝

5. *Why did God send such a horrific drought and famine upon the world? What were His purposes? What were His provisions?*

6. *What difficulties might Joseph have faced when he went from the bottom of society to the top so suddenly? What does this suggest about the importance of daily faithfulness to God?*

7. *What are the qualities of a godly leader? Of a submissive follower? How do the two overlap?*

8. *When have you seen God use someone in authority to bring blessing in your own life?*

⤳ Taking It Personally ⤳

9.   How well do you submit to authority figures? In what areas do you need to work on submission and respect toward authority?

10.   What practical lessons has the Lord taught you in times of hardship? How has He used those lessons in later situations?

RESCUING JACOB'S FAMILY

GENESIS 45, 46

ᔕ HISTORICAL BACKGROUND ᔕ

The seven years of famine had begun, and the whole world was flocking to Egypt to buy food, as we saw in the last study. Among that crowd of buyers were Joseph's ten brothers, who had sold him into Egyptian slavery more than twenty years earlier. (His youngest brother, Benjamin, remained behind with Jacob in Canaan.)

The first task Joseph needed to address was to bring about reconciliation with those brothers. We will examine that important process in Study 11. Once that was accomplished, he could set his mind on the joyful task of providing food for his starving family.

Joseph went far beyond merely providing food, though: he also provided a new home in the richest part of Egypt, and paid all moving expenses to get his entire family situated there. For the first time, the descendants of Abraham would have permanent homes rather than nomadic tents. (Those "permanent homes," it would turn out, would last some four hundred years before the Lord would call His people back to Canaan.)

Jacob was still living in Canaan at this period, dwelling in Hebron near the place where God had appeared to Abraham in Mamre (Genesis 18—see the map in the Introduction). He had already buried his beloved wife Rachel (Genesis 35:19), and it seems fairly likely that he had buried Leah, as well (see Genesis 49:30). We are not told whether his concubines, Zilpah and Bilhah, were still alive at this point, and it is entirely possible that they were. (Joseph's dream included both his father and mother bowing before him in Egypt, so it is quite possible that some of Jacob's wives joined him on that trip.) Regardless, Jacob was not lonely in Canaan, for his family had grown considerably, and he was surrounded with his daughters-in-law and numerous grandchildren—as well as his beloved son Benjamin.

The journey between Egypt and Hebron would take at least a week in each direction, and time would be required in Canaan to pack up and move the families and all their possessions back to Egypt. So Joseph provided many cartloads of food and provisions to nourish his family along the way—with far greater wealth awaiting them when they returned.

ᕤ READING GENESIS 45:16–28 ᕤ

PHARAOH REJOICES: *Word comes to Pharaoh that Joseph's brothers have arrived in Egypt, and he is so glad that he sends for Jacob's entire family.*

16. JOSEPH'S BROTHERS HAVE COME: It had been twenty-two years since Joseph's brothers had sold him into slavery. The seven years of plenty had come and gone, and the land was now in the midst of the seven years of famine. Much had transpired between Joseph and his brothers prior to this passage. The family had become fully reconciled, and Joseph had openly forgiven his brothers for their treachery. (See Study 11 for more on that reconciliation.)

18. BRING YOUR FATHER AND YOUR HOUSEHOLDS: Ten of Joseph's brothers were with him in Egypt, while their own families had remained behind in Canaan, along with Jacob and his youngest son, Benjamin.

I WILL GIVE YOU THE BEST OF THE LAND OF EGYPT: The story of Joseph began with deep tragedy, and most of Joseph's life to this point had been spent in suffering. But it was God's hand that had led each step of the way, and His plan was to bring about great goodness for His children, not to prolong suffering.

YOU WILL EAT THE FAT OF THE LAND: Abraham's descendants had lived for several generations as nomads in Canaan, dwelling in tents and moving from place to place. More recently, they had been struggling just to survive during a time of terrible famine—and suddenly they found themselves taken out of Canaan to live in the world's wealthiest land—as honored guests in the best of that land.

LAST TRIP TO CANAAN: *The brothers set forth on their last journey to Canaan to collect the remainder of their family. The people of Israel would not make this journey for another four hundred years.*

22. BUT TO BENJAMIN . . . : Joseph demonstrated special affection for his younger brother, Benjamin, because he was the only brother from the same mother, Rachel. This technically is not favoritism, since Joseph is merely one of the brothers rather than the father of the family, yet it is still worth noting that the other brothers did not exhibit any jealousy. This may indicate that true healing has taken place within the family.

24. SEE THAT YOU DO NOT BECOME TROUBLED ALONG THE WAY: The Hebrew word for *troubled* can mean "to tremble, rage, be agitated, be perturbed." Joseph was telling his brothers not to work themselves into an argument or fear concerning their sin against him, which happened long before. It is interesting that he commanded them to "see to it," to make a deliberate effort not to dredge up the past. Joseph wanted his brothers' sin to be buried and forgotten. He would later tell them, "But as for you, you meant evil against me; but God meant it for good, in order to bring it about as it is this day, to save many people alive" (Genesis 50:20). The brothers had behaved wickedly, yet the entire ordeal had been part of God's plan of deliverance, and Joseph wanted it to be forgiven and forgotten.

26. Jacob's heart stood still: It was incredible to Jacob to be told that his son was still alive, after firmly believing for more than twenty years that he was dead. It seemed too good to be true, but God's plans are always better than anything that we can hope for or imagine, for He "is able to do exceedingly abundantly above all that we ask or think, according to the power that works in us" (Ephesians 3:20).

Reading Genesis 46:1–7

Jacob Has a Vision: ***Jacob takes his family from Bethel to Beersheba, where he stops to worship. While there, the Lord appears in a vision.***

1. Beersheba: Jacob and his family had been living in Hebron (see the map in the Introduction). Abraham, Jacob's grandfather, had lived there for many years. Both Abraham and Isaac had built altars and publicly worshiped the Lord in Beersheba (Genesis 21:33; 26:23–25).

2. in the visions of the night: The Lord had given Jacob (also called Israel) another vision when he was in Bethel (Genesis 28:12–15), in which he saw a ladder or staircase ascending to heaven, and God's angels moving up and down. The Lord promised Jacob in that vision that He would be with him wherever he went, that his descendants would be as innumerable as the dust of the earth and would spread throughout the earth, and that his offspring would inherit the land of Canaan.

3. do not fear to go down to Egypt: The Lord here reiterated His promise that He would be with Jacob, even in Egypt—a promise He had clearly kept even throughout the sufferings of Joseph. He also repeated the promise "in your seed . . . all the families of the earth shall be blessed" (Genesis 28:14).

4. I will also surely bring you up again: The Lord had prophesied to Abraham that his descendants would be "strangers in a land that is not theirs," and that they would serve a foreign nation for four hundred years before returning to Canaan (Genesis 15:13–16). He had prophesied to Jacob, "I am with you and will keep you wherever you go, and will bring you back to this land; for I will not leave you until I have done what I have spoken to you" (Genesis 28:15). He was now letting Jacob know that this journey into Egypt was the beginning of fulfillment of those prophecies.

Joseph will put his hand on your eyes: That is, Jacob would finish his days in peace, and would die in the company of his beloved son Joseph.

6. Jacob and all his descendants with him: Thus, Joseph's second dream was finally brought to pass, as his father and whole family came to Egypt and bowed themselves before his authority (see Genesis 37:9).

↶ First Impressions ↷

1. Why did Pharaoh rejoice so extravagantly when Joseph's brothers came to Egypt? What does this reveal about Joseph's character?

2. If you had been in Jacob's place, how would you have responded when told that your son—whom you thought to be dead—was alive? And in command of all Egypt?

3. *Why did Joseph give Benjamin so much more than the rest of his brothers? How would you have felt in Benjamin's place? In Joseph's place?*

4. *Why did Joseph warn his brothers not to "become troubled" on their way back to Canaan? What does this reveal of Joseph's wisdom?*

↳ Some Key Principles ↰

God's prophetic words always come to pass.

The Lord prophesied to Abraham that his descendants would one day journey to a foreign land where they would serve their masters for approximately four hundred years, after which time they would return to Canaan. Abraham, however, never saw any part of that prophecy come to pass, nor did his son Isaac. In fact, it took several hundred years just for the first part to transpire, when Jacob's entire family finally moved to Egypt.

Abraham, Isaac, Jacob, and Joseph all knew the Lord's promises concerning His plans, but none of them knew the timetable or methods God would use to accomplish those plans—yet they all lived their lives believing in the truth of His promises. The

Lord used the wickedness of men to place His servant in the right position at the right time, yet His servant Joseph did not know, even in the midst of it, that the Lord was doing so to bring about His prophecies.

God always keeps His promises, but He rarely tells us exactly how those promises will come to pass. It is our part, as God's children, to rest in faith that He will keep His Word, and to remain faithful to the things that He has commanded us to do in the meantime.

The Lord always provides for His people.

The famine and drought in Egypt and Canaan were very severe, and it is likely that many people died from its deprivations. Yet all of Jacob's household survived—in fact, they more than survived; they thrived when the world around them was in want.

That famine did not catch God by surprise; He ordained it as part of His plan to move Israel into Egypt in preparation for their exodus into the promised land of Canaan. He saw all things that would transpire in the future, even to the end of time, and He had planned from before the beginning of time exactly how He would prove His faithfulness to His people.

Sometimes, however, His provision required that some of His people suffer. Joseph suffered grievously prior to being elevated to the leadership of Egypt, and it is likely that he wondered at times whether God had forgotten him. But the Lord had not forgotten Joseph, or any others in the family of Israel, and He proved it by providing for all their needs. He never forgets His promises or His children.

We may experience sorrow for a time, but joy will certainly follow.

Both Jacob and Joseph experienced times of great sorrow in their lives. Joseph endured slavery and life in prison for several years; Jacob spent many years grieving that his favorite son was dead. But both men experienced joy and blessings which far outweighed those sorrows.

The Lord permits sorrow and hardship to enter the lives of His children from time to time, and when we are in the midst of those trials it can be hard to see any joy that might result. Yet the Lord proved His sovereignty over all the circumstances of Joseph's life, and He is still sovereign today over the affairs of our lives. He permits both blessings and sorrows to enter our lives for the express purpose of making us more like Christ, "and we know that all things work together for good to those who love God, to those who are the called according to His purpose" (Romans 8:28).

"My brethren, count it all joy when you fall into various trials, knowing that the testing of your faith produces patience. But let patience have its perfect work, that you may be perfect and complete, lacking nothing" (James 1:2–4). "Sing praise to the LORD, you saints of His, and give thanks at the remembrance of His holy name. For His anger is but for a moment, His favor is for life; weeping may endure for a night, but joy comes in the morning" (Psalm 30:4–5).

⤳ DIGGING DEEPER ⤳

5. If you had been one of Joseph's ten brothers, how would you have reacted to Joseph's generosity?

6. How might the ten brothers have felt as they journeyed back to Canaan? How might they have felt when explaining to Jacob what really happened to Joseph?

7. List below all the circumstances and events that the Lord used in Joseph's life to bring about this great provision for his family. What does this reveal about His sovereignty?

8. List below some prophecies of Scripture that have not yet been completely fulfilled. How should these prophecies affect your life today?

⤳ TAKING IT PERSONALLY ⤳

9. When have you seen the Lord's generous provision in your own life? When have you struggled in times of deprivation?

10. Are you building your life today on the promises of God? Do you truly believe what the Bible says concerning the future?

SECTION 2:

CHARACTERS

In This Section:

— 6 —
Joseph As a Picture of Christ

↳ Character's Background ↲

The New Testament does not specifically treat Joseph as a type of Christ, yet his life presented many parallels that can provide us with helpful illustrations of the character and work of Jesus. We have already considered some of these elements in previous studies; we will look at more in this study.

One of the major themes in Joseph's life is his debasement to the lowest stratum of humanity in Egypt, where he suffered as a slave and a prisoner, followed by a sudden and dramatic elevation to the right hand of Pharaoh. In a sense, this parallels the ministry of Jesus Christ, who lowered Himself from the right hand of God in order to be born in a stable, grow up in a carpenter's house, preach a message that would be rejected by the religious leaders, wash the feet of His disciples, and suffer the most debased form of death on a cross. Yet He is now seated on high at the right hand of the Father, and the day is coming when His glory shall be fully revealed on earth, and every knee shall bow and every tongue confess that Jesus Christ is Lord.

Joseph's life provides further illustrations of Jesus, in his constant attitude of humility and submission to the will of his various masters—including Potiphar, the prison supervisor, and Pharaoh himself. His focus was always on obedience to God, and he trusted fully in God's sovereignty over all of his circumstances.

We will return to the time when Joseph was sold into slavery by his brothers, and then follow his steps through Potiphar's house to the house of Pharaoh. Though we will be reviewing some of the passages we have examined in previous studies, this time we will look specifically for the ways that Joseph's life reflects and foreshadows the character of Jesus.

LOVED BY THE FATHER: *Joseph enjoyed full fellowship with his father, and his father delighted to demonstrate his love.*

3. ISRAEL LOVED JOSEPH: Joseph's sufferings also afflicted his father, who loved him with unique and unparalleled affection. In a similar way, God the Father underwent much sorrow on our behalf when He sent His only begotten and beloved Son to die on the cross.

4. THEY HATED HIM: Jesus taught a parable about a rich landowner who rented his vineyards to some tenants. But when he sent his servants to collect some of the fruit, the tenants beat them and stoned them and even murdered them. "Then last of all he sent his son to them, saying, 'They will respect my son.' But when the vinedressers saw the son, they said among themselves, 'This is the heir. Come, let us kill him and seize his inheritance.' So they took him and cast him out of the vineyard and killed him'" (Matthew 21:37–39).

5. JOSEPH HAD A DREAM . . . AND THEY HATED HIM EVEN MORE: The world also hates Jesus because of His claims that He is the only way to God (John 14:6), and His promise that He will one day rule over all creation (Revelation 21).

13. I WILL SEND YOU TO THEM: Similarly, the Father sent His beloved Son to earth—for the specific purpose of dying on the cross.

HERE I AM: Joseph demonstrated a submissive attitude throughout his life. He was always ready to obey his father, and was equally loyal and submissive to his masters in Egypt. In this, he pictures the obedience of Christ, who submitted Himself completely to the will of His Father in all things—even to death on the cross.

JEALOUSY REARS ITS UGLY HEAD: *Joseph's brothers resented him, and they had already rejected the idea that he would one day rule over them. Now they put that resentment into action.*

18. THEY CONSPIRED AGAINST HIM TO KILL HIM: Jesus suffered in a similar manner. "Then the chief priests, the scribes, and the elders of the people assembled at the palace of the high priest, who was called Caiaphas, and plotted to take Jesus by trickery and kill Him" (Matthew 26:3–4). "Then, from that day on, they plotted to put Him to death" (John 11:53).

19. LOOK, THIS DREAMER IS COMING: The religious leaders thought Jesus was a dreamer, too. "So the Jews answered and said to Him, 'What sign do You show to us, since You do these things?' Jesus answered and said to them, 'Destroy this temple, and in three days I will raise it up.' Then the Jews said, 'It has taken forty-six years to build this temple, and will You raise it up in three days?' But He was speaking of the temple of His body" (John 2:18–21).

23. THEY STRIPPED JOSEPH OF HIS TUNIC: Again, this scene is hauntingly familiar. "Then they crucified Him, and divided His garments, casting lots, that it might be fulfilled which was spoken by the prophet: 'They divided My garments among them, and for My clothing they cast lots'" (Matthew 27:35).

25. THEY SAT DOWN TO EAT A MEAL: The callous behavior of the brothers, sitting and calmly eating lunch while Joseph wept in the pit below, is reminiscent of those who stood at the foot of the cross and mocked the Savior. "He saved others; Himself He cannot save. If He is the King of Israel, let Him now come down from the cross, and we will believe Him" (Matthew 27:42).

28. SOLD HIM TO THE ISHMAELITES FOR TWENTY SHEKELS OF SILVER: In a similar manner, Judas "sold" Jesus to the religious leaders for thirty pieces of silver: "Then one of the twelve, called Judas Iscariot, went to the chief priests and said, 'What are you willing to give me if I deliver Him to you?' And they counted out to him thirty pieces of silver ... Then was fulfilled what was spoken by Jeremiah the prophet, saying, 'And they took the thirty pieces of silver, the value of Him who was priced'" (Matthew 26:14; 27:9).

᚛ READING GENESIS 39:1–20 ᚜

DOWN INTO EGYPT: *Joseph did not debase himself to a servant's position voluntarily, as Jesus did, yet his attitude during slavery presents a compelling picture of Christ as the humble servant.*

1. JOSEPH HAD BEEN TAKEN DOWN TO EGYPT: The Son of God, like Joseph, was also taken to Egypt. "An angel of the Lord appeared to Joseph [the husband of Jesus' mother, Mary] in a dream, saying, 'Arise, take the young Child and His mother, flee to Egypt, and stay there until I bring you word; for Herod will seek the young Child to destroy Him.' When he arose, he took the young Child and His mother by night and departed for Egypt, and was there until the death of Herod, that it might be fulfilled which was spoken by the Lord through the prophet, saying, 'Out of Egypt I called My Son'" (Matthew 2:13–15).

3. THE LORD MADE ALL HE DID TO PROSPER IN HIS HAND: Joseph was obviously endowed with God-given wisdom, both spiritual and commercial. Compare this description to Luke's portrayal of Christ: "And the Child grew and became strong in spirit, filled with wisdom; and the grace of God was upon Him" (Luke 2:40).

9. How then can I do this great wickedness, and sin against God? : When faced with temptation, Joseph took a strong stand against it. Jesus also faced temptation at the hands of Satan, and He, too, stood firm against it. Like Joseph, Jesus understood that all sin is ultimately against God. He resisted the devil's wiles by focusing on the Word of God.

14. he has brought in to us a Hebrew to mock us: The Jews also used this false accusation against Jesus, suggesting to their Roman rulers that Jesus was leading a rebellion against Rome (see John 19:12).

20. put him into the prison: Jesus was bound and taken captive to stand before Pilate. But whereas Joseph found favor in the eyes of his captors, Jesus did not. He was mocked, scourged, beaten—and executed.

↶ Reading Genesis 41:38–45 ↷

Elevated to Honor and Authority: *Joseph is suddenly swept from the lowest level of society to the height of authority. Jesus, too, was raised to sit at the right hand of the Father.*

38. a man in whom is the Spirit of God: Thousands of years later, a physician turned historian would write: "And [Jesus] was handed the book of the prophet Isaiah. And when He had opened the book, He found the place where it was written: '*The Spirit of the Lord is upon me, because He has anointed me to preach the gospel to the poor; He has sent me to heal the brokenhearted, to proclaim liberty to the captives and recovery of sight to the blind, to set at liberty those who are oppressed; to proclaim the acceptable year of the Lord.*' Then He closed the book, and gave it back to the attendant and sat down. And the eyes of all who were in the synagogue were fixed on Him. And He began to say to them, '*Today this Scripture is fulfilled in your hearing*'" (Luke 4:17–21).

41. I have set you over all the land of Egypt: Joseph was elevated to "the right hand" of Pharaoh, giving him the authority to speak on Pharaoh's behalf. The New Testament shows us that Jesus is seated at "the right hand of God" (Acts 2:33): "Therefore being exalted to the right hand of God, and having received from the Father the promise of the Holy Spirit, He poured out this which you now see and hear. For David did not ascend into the heavens, but he says himself: '*The Lord said to my Lord, "Sit at my right hand, till i make your enemies your footstool.*' Therefore let all the house of Israel know assuredly that God has made this Jesus, whom you crucified, both Lord and Christ" (Acts 2:33–36). "But to which of the angels has He ever said: '*Sit at my right hand, till i make your enemies your footstool'?*" (Hebrews 1:13).

42. HIS SIGNET RING: This ring gave Joseph the authority to make official decrees on Pharaoh's behalf. Similarly, Jesus' words reflected the authority of His Father. "He who has seen Me has seen the Father; so how can you say, 'Show us the Father'? Do you not believe that I am in the Father, and the Father in Me? The words that I speak to you I do not speak on My own authority; but the Father who dwells in Me does the works" (John 14:9–10).

43. BOW THE KNEE!: All of Egypt was compelled to bow before Joseph. Now listen to the words of Paul: "That at the name of Jesus every knee should bow, of those in heaven, and of those on earth, and of those under the earth, and that every tongue should confess that Jesus Christ is Lord, to the glory of God the Father" (Philippians 2:10–11).

ᕯ FIRST IMPRESSIONS ᕮ

1. *What special privileges did Joseph enjoy under his father's care? What privileges did the Son of God enjoy prior to becoming a man?*

2. *Why did Joseph become a slave? Why did Jesus humble Himself to become a servant?*

3. *In what ways did Jacob suffer when his son was sold into slavery? What did it cost God the Father to send His Son to die on the cross?*

4. *How do the actions of Joseph's brothers illustrate the attitude of those who reject Christ?*

⌒ Some Key Principles ⌒

Jesus was the suffering Servant.

Jesus is the only begotten Son of God, and He enjoyed perfect fellowship with the Father in heaven. Yet He willingly forsook that glorious position in order to wash the feet of sinful men. More significantly, He gave up the glories of heaven in order to be nailed to a cross, the most degrading and torturous form of death at the time.

Joseph presents a very imperfect image of this, as he was sold into slavery against his will. Yet his attitude as a slave, and later as a prisoner, reflect the humble servanthood of Jesus. Joseph did not argue or try to escape his slavery; rather, he willingly undertook whatever menial task he was given to do. In the same way, Jesus did not hesitate to perform the most menial task of all, bending low to wash the feet of His followers.

Jesus calls His followers today to imitate that example, serving one another in love and humility. If the Lord of lords Himself was willing to kneel and wash His disciples' feet, then there should not be *any* form of loving service that we consider beneath our dignity.

Jesus sought the will of the Father in all things.

Joseph resisted the advances of Potiphar's wife because his focus was on God rather than on himself or his surroundings. Jesus resisted the temptations of the devil because His focus was on pleasing His Father, and He drew strength from the written Word of God.

Joseph found himself far from home as a captive, enslaved in another man's household, yet he did not try to escape, but instead accepted his situation as God's will and submitted himself under the burden of suffering. Jesus faced a far greater burden of suffering when He prayed in the garden of Gethsemane, anticipating a dreadful death on the cross and a temporary separation from God. Yet He did not try to escape from that, but submitted Himself to the Father's will, "saying, 'Father, if it is Your will, take this cup away from Me; nevertheless not My will, but Yours, be done'" (Luke 22:42).

Christians are commanded to follow this example. Our highest priority is to obey the will of God. "Not everyone who says to Me, 'Lord, Lord,' shall enter the kingdom of heaven, but he who does the will of My Father in heaven" (Matthew 7:21).

Jesus is seated at the right hand of the Father, and will one day return in all His glory.

Imagine the dramatic change that swept Joseph from the pits of prison onto the highest throne in the world's most powerful nation—all in one day! Yet this dramatic elevation is nothing compared with the glory of Jesus Christ, who burst out of the tomb and was lifted to the highest heights of heaven.

Joseph's story did not end with his promotion; his greatest work was still before him, as he saved the known world from a dreadful famine and prepared a new home for God's chosen people. The story of Jesus' work of redemption and lordship did not end at the cross, or even at His resurrection and ascension into heaven. The best part is still to come!

The day is approaching, and may well be very near, when Jesus Himself "will descend from heaven with a shout, with the voice of an archangel, and with the trumpet of God. And the dead in Christ will rise first. Then we who are alive and remain shall be caught up together with them in the clouds to meet the Lord in the air. And thus we shall always be with the Lord" (1 Thessalonians 4:16–17). Christians should live each day in anticipation of that great event.

5. How did Joseph's life provide a picture of Jesus as the suffering servant? In what ways was the humility of Jesus far greater than that of Joseph or any other human being?

6. Give some specific examples of how Joseph submitted himself to the sovereignty of God. Give some specific examples of how Jesus did the same.

7. When Joseph was elevated in Egypt, he provided a new home for his family. What blessings does Jesus provide for His followers from His seat at the Father's right hand?

8. How frequently do you reflect on the return of Christ? Does that imminent event influence the way that you live?

9. Do you frequently consider that your circumstances have been ordained by God? How does God's sovereignty affect your present circumstances?

10. Are there areas of service to others that you avoid? How might the Lord be calling you to serve others this week?

~ 7 ~
JUDAH

GENESIS 38, 42, 43

ᕤ HISTORICAL BACKGROUND ᕤ

We will now return to the time when Joseph was first sent into Egyptian slavery. He had been wrenched from his family against his will, but his brother Judah would leave the family voluntarily in hopes of personal gain. Judah surrounded himself with Canaanite friends, and even took a Canaanite wife—disregarding his family's injunctions against intermarriage.

Judah's move to Canaan highlights the danger that Israel faced: if left in Canaan, they might well have intermarried and drifted from God's special calling to be separated to Him. The Lord forced Jacob to move his family to Egypt, in part to preserve them from that danger. (The family was forced to live apart from the Egyptians, who did not want anything to do with them.)

We have seen previously that Reuben had lost his rights as firstborn due to sin (Genesis 35:22), and both Simeon and Levi had also forfeited that right (see Study 4). The next in line was Judah, but in this chapter we will see that he, too, was unqualified to be the family's spiritual leader. Fortunately, God's grace overrides man's sin, and He can turn even our own failures into His glory. As we will see, God was at work in Judah's life to prepare him for his role as leader in his family—and ultimately to bring His own Son into the world through Judah's descendants.

ᕤ READING GENESIS 38:1–29 ᕤ

JUDAH LEAVES HOME: *Joseph was forced to leave his family against his will, but his brother Judah chose to leave for his own profit.*

1. AT THAT TIME: The events in this chapter took place around the time when Joseph was sold into Egypt—perhaps while he was still in Potiphar's household. Joseph's response to Potiphar's wife would present a stark contrast to Judah's behavior here.

Judah departed from his brothers: Judah evidently left his family altogether and moved to a nearby Canaanite town. He was effectively turning his back on the teaching of Abraham, Isaac, and Jacob. Here we see a distinction between himself and his brother Joseph, who had been separated from his family by force, while Judah did so of his own accord.

Adullamite: Adullam was a town near Hebron.

Preserving a Heritage: *Judah took a Canaanite wife, then watched his sons die for their wickedness. He feared that his lineage would be cut off.*

2. he married her: Abraham and Isaac had both made it clear to their sons that they were not to marry Canaanite women (Genesis 24:3; 28:1), but Judah deliberately ignored the injunction.

6. Judah took a wife for Er: We know little about Tamar, the woman whom Judah selected to marry his son, but it is likely that she was also a Canaanite. Had the Lord permitted the sons of Jacob to remain in Canaan, they would have become indistinguishable from the world around them within a few generations.

8. raise up an heir to your brother: The Mosaic law would later codify this practice, known as a levirate marriage. If a man died without an heir, his brother was expected to marry the widow and produce an heir for his dead brother. (See Deuteronomy 25:5–10.) This is what Judah was requesting of his son Onan, because Er had died.

9. But Onan knew that the heir would not be his: Onan's firstborn son would, in fact, take the name of Er and would be considered Er's heir rather than Onan's, according to the levirate marital practices.

he emitted on the ground, lest he should give an heir to his brother: Onan's attitude was completely self-serving, and he refused to look after his late brother's heritage. His behavior is reminiscent of Cain, who insisted that he was not his "brother's keeper" (Genesis 4:9).

11. Lest he also die like his brothers: Judah had lost two sons during his sojourn in Canaan, and he would have no heir if he lost his third son, Shelah, so he told Er's widow to wait until this son grew up, knowing very well that Shelah would never marry her.

Indulging the Flesh: *Some time later, Judah hired a prostitute. He didn't know, however, that she was his own daughter-in-law.*

12. Timnah: This Canaanite city would also prove a snare to Samson, who took a Canaanite wife there. (See Judges 14.)

13. shear his sheep: Sheep-shearing time was renowned in the Canaanite culture for its festivities and licentious behavior. The pagan cultures worshipped many false gods, and they practiced fertility rites during sheep shearing and harvest.

14. covered herself with a veil and wrapped herself: Tamar deliberately disguised herself as a prostitute, evidently intending to trap Judah. This suggests that she had little respect for Judah's character.

she was not given to him as a wife: It was a disgrace in that culture for a woman to have no children, and the name and heritage of her first husband, Er, would be wiped out if she remained a childless widow. Judah had deceived Tamar into believing that she would become the wife of Shelah, so she took desperate measures to address the problem. Some ancient pagan laws carried the levirate marriage responsibility as far as the father-in-law, and it is possible that Tamar expected Judah himself to marry her.

16. Please let me come in to you: Judah demonstrated that Tamar's opinion of his moral character was correct, as he initiated the sin.

18. Your signet and cord, and your staff: It was customary to require three forms of "identification" in ratifying a contract in that culture. The signet was probably a cylinder that Judah wore on a cord around his neck, used to endorse legal documents. His staff was probably unique in some way, such that it was easily recognizable as his personal property (v. 25).

23. lest we be shamed: It was certainly not good for Judah's reputation to go about town asking the whereabouts of a local prostitute, so he dropped the issue. The sad irony is, however, that his shameful deed would be found out far more dramatically than he anticipated.

I sent this young goat: Judah may have thought that the shame of his action was in not paying the prostitute. He evidently felt that he had fulfilled his responsibility by making concerted efforts to pay her, and evidently he thought no more about it.

24. let her be burned: Judah's hypocrisy is astounding here, as he demanded that his daughter-in-law be burned to death for prostituting herself, without giving any thought to his own apparent habit of hiring prostitutes himself.

26. She has been more righteous than I: Judah was not endorsing Tamar's deeds; he was acknowledging that she had been attentive to proper inheritance rights, which he had blatantly ignored. He also was smitten with the confrontation of his own sinful behavior, and recognized his hypocrisy. This may have been a turning point in Judah's life; we will see as we go along that he became a responsible man—and indeed he is in the genealogy of Jesus Himself.

29. Perez: Meaning "breach" or "pushing through." It is interesting to note that the genealogy of Jesus is traced through Perez, not through Judah's legitimate son Shelah. God in His grace can turn even our sinful acts to His glory.

⌁ Reading Genesis 42:36–38; 43:1–13 ⌁

A Ransom for Benjamin: *Joseph sent his brothers to get Benjamin, but Jacob refused to let him go. Both Reuben and Judah offered solutions, but only Judah's offer was acceptable.*

42:36. you want to take Benjamin: Joseph had sent his brothers back to Canaan during their first visit to Egypt in order to bring Benjamin to him.

37. Reuben spoke to his father: Reuben was the firstborn, and ordinarily would have been the leader for his brothers. But his earlier sin (Genesis 35:22) had removed him from that position, in God's eyes, and his leadership had become ineffective.

Kill my two sons: This was a bold suggestion, and Reuben undoubtedly meant it as a firm sign of his commitment to protect Benjamin. Judah, however, would later offer a better ransom: his own life.

38. My son shall not go down with you: Reuben's leadership failed. The Lord had already chosen another to succeed him in the role of firstborn.

43:1. the famine was severe in the land: As already stated, this was during the brothers' trips to Egypt at the time of the famine, prior to Jacob's permanent move there.

3. Judah spoke to him: Judah was beginning to take up his role as the firstborn, taking leadership of his brothers.

9. I myself will be surety for him: Judah offered himself as ransom for Benjamin's life, in contrast to Reuben's offer of his sons.

13. Take your brother also: Judah's leadership was effective, unlike Reuben's.

⌁ Reading Genesis 44:14–34 ⌁

Making Himself a Ransom: *Judah offers himself as a pledge for Benjamin's safety.*

14. JUDAH AND HIS BROTHERS: It is interesting that Judah was now listed first, as the recognized leader in his family. The Lord had placed upon him the responsibilities of the firstborn, and he had grown in godliness to the point that he fulfilled that role.

16. GOD HAS FOUND OUT THE INIQUITY OF YOUR SERVANTS: Judah had been confronted with the sins of the brothers against Joseph, and he had repented. This was what Joseph was looking for, as we will see in Study 11—the repentance of his brothers, and the reconciliation of his family.

17. HE SHALL BE MY SLAVE: Joseph was testing his brothers, offering them a chance to redeem themselves at the expense of their innocent brother. They had sinned in this way once before, and it must have been a tempting offer.

31. HE WILL DIE: The brothers had not cared about Jacob's grief when they attempted to murder Joseph. But Judah and his brothers had since repented of that sin, and they were determined not to grieve their father any further.

33. LET YOUR SERVANT REMAIN INSTEAD OF THE LAD: Judah made good on his offer and was fully prepared to stand in the place of his brother, becoming a slave in Egypt.

ᕦ FIRST IMPRESSIONS ᕤ

1.   *Why did Tamar ensnare Judah in sexual sin? Why did Judah commit that sin?*

2.   *What did Judah reveal about his character when he ordered Tamar to be burned? What was he most concerned about in that situation?*

3.   *How were the ransoms of Reuben and Judah different? What did their offers reveal of their respective characters?*

4. *In what ways did Judah change over the course of these passages? How did the Lord use his failures to teach him godly character?*

⌁ Some Key Principles ⌁

Our sin can hinder God's blessings in our lives.

Reuben was Jacob's firstborn son and would have naturally received the inheritance blessing. This would have placed on his shoulders the responsibility of leading his family and acting as the spiritual head—but his sin with his father's concubine effectively removed him from that position.

Reuben was not disinherited from Jacob's family, but he did lose some tremendous blessings that would have been his. A Christian does not lose his salvation when he sins, but he may very well deprive himself of God's greatest blessings in his life.

God's greatest gift to His children is eternal life in His presence, but He goes far beyond that gift, working to pour out upon us "every spiritual blessing in the heavenly places in Christ" (Ephesians 1:3). We hinder those blessings, however, when we stray from obedience to God's Word.

God can use even our failures to His glory.

Our sin can hinder God's blessings in our lives, as we have already seen, yet God continues to work in our lives—despite our failures—to make us more like His Son. Judah was no less guilty of sin than his brothers, yet the Lord worked faithfully to change his character and make him fit for service.

The Scriptures are filled with men and women who were imperfect, who fell into sin—some of them grievous sins—while God continued to work in their lives. David, for example, committed adultery and murder, yet the Lord did not abandon him. Both Judah and David were in the genealogical line of Jesus.

The key to this is not in living a sinless life, but in repenting of sin each time we fail. David demonstrated a heart for God when he acknowledged his sin and turned away from it, just as Judah demonstrated a change of character by offering himself as ransom for Benjamin. God will always accept a penitent heart, and He will turn our failures into His glory.

Jesus gave Himself as a ransom for our sins.

In an extended sense, Judah presented a picture of Christ—His future descendant—when he offered to give his own life in exchange for his brother Benjamin. Yet this picture was imperfect, because Benjamin had done nothing to deserve becoming a slave in Egypt—whereas Judah had!

Jesus lived a perfect, sinless life in complete submission to the Father's will, yet He gave His life willingly on the cross in order to redeem us from our guilt: "The Son of Man did not come to be served, but to serve, and to give His life a ransom for many" (Matthew 20:28). "For there is one God and one Mediator between God and men, the Man Christ Jesus, who gave Himself a ransom for all" (1 Timothy 2:5–6). No man or woman in the history of the world has been worthy of this ransom; every one of us stood guilty before God, deserving His full wrath against sin.

⤳ DIGGING DEEPER ⤲

5. *What do we learn of God's grace from the sordid affair of Judah and Tamar? How did the Lord bring glory to Himself through Judah's sin?*

6. *What would have happened to Abraham's descendants if they had remained in Canaan? Why was it necessary for God to incubate them in Egypt?*

7. Consider the family of Jacob. How did sin produce bad consequences in their individual lives? How did Joseph present a stark contrast?

8. What changed in Judah's heart to make him willing to be a ransom for Benjamin?

ᕗ Taking It Personally ᕫ

9. When have you seen God's glory come out of someone's failures? How have you seen His grace at work in your own life?

10. Is there sin in your life that is hindering God's full blessing? What changes in your heart might the Lord be asking you to make?

8

Pharaoh's Chief Butler

Genesis 40, 41

Historical Background

We will now return to the time when Joseph was thrown into prison by Potiphar, which we examined in Study 3. He was in prison under a false accusation for many years, and there appeared little hope of his ever being exonerated and set free. But Joseph never lost heart, because he knew that the Lord was in control of all his circumstances, and he trusted that God would fulfill the prophecies of his youthful dreams (Genesis 37).

Meanwhile, as Joseph worked diligently in the prison house, two men of high rank in Pharaoh's court had some problems of their own. We are not told what provoked the king's anger, but something serious evidently occurred. The chief butler and chief baker were personally responsible for everything that Pharaoh ate and drank. This included the weighty responsibility of ensuring that nobody tried to poison the king. It is quite possible that such an attempt was made, or that some political intrigue was uncovered at court, because the king evidently held one of these two men responsible.

It might have taken some time for Pharaoh to sort out who was responsible and who was guilty, for the chief butler and chief baker sat in prison for about a year. By the time they were released, however, the king had arrived at a conclusion: one of them was innocent; the other must die. Joseph knew nothing of these intrigues, of course, yet he would become a very important player in the drama.

Fortunately for all concerned, God was still in control.

Reading Genesis 40:1–23

Pharaoh Is Angry: *Joseph is in prison as this chapter opens, placed there after Potiphar's wife falsely accused him.*

1. after these things: These events occurred sometime after Joseph had been thrown into prison by Potiphar. He had probably been in prison for a fair amount of time, since the prison warden had already come to trust him implicitly.

THE BUTLER AND THE BAKER: These were men of high authority and responsibility in Pharaoh's court, despite their humble-sounding titles. The chief butler was the king's personal cupbearer, responsible for anything that Pharaoh drank. The chief baker was responsible for the king's bread—and both men had to be completely trustworthy and beyond the influence of Pharaoh's enemies.

2. PHARAOH WAS ANGRY: We are not told what these two men had done, or whether they were even guilty of any crime. The end result for the chief baker, however, would suggest that the king might have suspected these two men of disloyalty. Since each had the potential of poisoning him, Pharaoh could not take chances.

3. CAPTAIN OF THE GUARD: This may well have been Potiphar, who was called the captain of the guard (Genesis 39:1). If so, it is likely that he placed Joseph in charge of these two important prisoners because Joseph had already proven himself trustworthy.

JOSEPH THE SERVANT: *We have already considered Joseph's servant spirit in Study 3, but here we see that he has not lost his focus—despite a seemingly hopeless situation.*

4. HE SERVED THEM: Service was a hallmark of Joseph's life. He made it a practice to put the concerns of others before his own. This will become apparent in this chapter, and it is the very characteristic that placed Joseph in a position to be elevated to Pharaoh's right hand.

THEY WERE IN CUSTODY FOR A WHILE: Joseph was probably in prison for many years.

5. DREAM: God had given Joseph the ability to interpret prophetic dreams, the very ability that convinced Pharaoh to place him in authority some time later. Yet it must have been a bitter reminder to Joseph of his own prophetic dream, finding himself in prison, interpreting the dreams of other men, when his dream had predicted a position of authority for himself. It is remarkable that this young man never gave way to bitterness or despair, but always waited for God to prove Himself faithful.

6. JOSEPH CAME IN TO THEM IN THE MORNING: He probably waited on these important men daily, serving them as their own private butler. It must have seemed ironic to the chief butler, many years later, to have the roles reversed.

SAW THAT THEY WERE SAD: Here we see Joseph's servant spirit in action. If anyone had reason to be sad in that prison, it was Joseph, who was there because of a false accusation by a powerful woman—indeed, he was there because of a terrible betrayal by his own brothers. But Joseph was not consumed by his woes, and was, instead, quick to show compassion for another person's suffering, even if that suffering was nothing compared to his own.

7. Why do you look so sad today? : A more common response might have been, "You think *you* have problems?!" But Joseph was genuinely concerned to serve these men and to do anything in his power to remove their sorrow.

8. Do not interpretations belong to God? : Joseph recognized God as the source of the understanding of all dreams.

13. Pharaoh will lift up your head: There is some ironic word play in this phrase. It can mean that Pharaoh will bestow great honor upon him (as in this case), or it can mean that Pharaoh will lift up his head quite literally—remove it, in fact, as with the chief baker.

14. remember me when it is well with you: This is the only record that we have of Joseph looking after his own interests, and it shows both restraint and wisdom on his part. He had not asked for anything in return for his service to the chief butler, always placing the interests of others above his own. But he also took advantage of a legitimate opportunity to request help in undoing the injustice.

Butler and Baker: *The dreams themselves give us some insight into the characters of these two men. One is a faithful servant, the other just self-serving.*

16. the chief baker saw that the interpretation was good: This gives us a bit of understanding regarding the chief baker's character. He evidently was not interested in having Joseph interpret his dream unless he could be confident that the interpretation was good. He seems to have been more concerned with personal gain than with learning truth.

I also was in my dream: Here is another subtle insight into this man's nature. He saw himself as the center point of his dream—"I was in my dream"—whereas the chief butler saw the vine as the centerpiece (v. 9).

17. the birds ate them: The two dreams themselves give us a picture of these two men. In the chief baker's dream, he was careless of his responsibility before Pharaoh, allowing birds to eat the bread right off his head. The chief butler's dream, by contrast, showed him thinking of his master at all times, finding a succulent vine and making wine for Pharaoh. The dreams suggest that the chief butler was a faithful servant, while the chief baker was not.

19. Pharoah will . . . hang you on a tree: Apparently the chief baker was beheaded, and his corpse was either hung from a tree branch or gallows, or else impaled. It was a sign of utter disgrace.

20. Pharaoh's birthday: Archaeology substantiates that Pharaoh would release political prisoners on his birthday.

23. THE CHIEF BUTLER DID NOT REMEMBER JOSEPH: He completely forgot him, despite the service Joseph had performed. This suggests that the chief butler's faithfulness was limited: he was a faithful servant to Pharaoh, but disregarded those beneath his social caste. Joseph, on the other hand, was faithful to any task the Lord placed before him, and he served both high and low equally.

⤙ READING GENESIS 41:1–14 ⤚

THE BUTLER REMEMBERS: *Joseph languished in prison for another two years, waiting for the chief butler to help him. It took Pharaoh's intervention to jog his memory.*

1. AT THE END OF TWO FULL YEARS: By that time, most people would assume that they had been completely forgotten and abandoned. From a human perspective, there was no hope that Joseph would ever get out of prison alive. But God was about to prove Himself faithful to His servant.

PHARAOH HAD A DREAM: See Study 4 for further information on Pharaoh's dreams.

8. THE MAGICIANS OF EGYPT: These were probably astrologers and practitioners of other pagan mysteries. Moses would also confront them when the time came for Israel to leave Egypt—and the Lord's power was proven to be the only source of truth in both instances.

9. I REMEMBER MY FAULTS THIS DAY: The chief butler may have been an opportunist, conveniently remembering Joseph only when it might prove profitable to himself, yet his confession of fault does seem sincere.

14. PHARAOH SENT AND CALLED JOSEPH: Joseph's faithful service at last received its reward: he was suddenly released from prison. Yet God's purposes were far greater than merely restoring Joseph's freedom, as we have seen in previous studies, and He had deliberately trained Joseph for his position of authority and placed him in a position—albeit in prison—where he could be ready to take charge.

⤙ FIRST IMPRESSIONS ⤚

1. *If you had been in Joseph's place, how would you have felt as a prison slave? How would you have reacted to the butler and baker's sadness?*

2. If you had been in the butler's place, how would you have responded to Joseph's interpretation of your dream? How would you have responded in the baker's place?

3. What can we infer about the butler and baker from their respective dreams?

4. Why do you think the butler forgot Joseph? How might he have felt when he saw Joseph raised to Pharaoh's right hand?

⤳ Some Key Principles ⤝

God's people should be ready and willing to serve in all situations.

Joseph had been treacherously treated by many people, including his own brothers, in situations where he was completely innocent of any wrongdoing. He had languished in prison for several years under a false accusation, and had little hope of ever being released. It would be understandable if he had sulked and looked after his own interests in such a situation.

But that is not how Joseph responded. When he found an opportunity to serve others, he did so willingly and cheerfully. The concerns of the chief butler were puny compared to Joseph's, yet Joseph did not chide him for sulking over a strange dream.

Jesus Christ is another example of one who never missed an opportunity to serve others—even though He is the Creator of the universe. He humbled Himself before His disciples when He washed their feet, and He submitted Himself to a horrible death on the cross. As His followers, Christians are also called to serve one another cheerfully and freely.

Remember those who have helped you in the past.

The chief butler had a tremendously important position in Pharaoh's court, and he was probably responsible for a full staff of assistants—to say nothing of the health and welfare of the king. The cares and duties of his career probably crowded Joseph out of his mind. Nevertheless, he had a responsibility to demonstrate his gratitude for Joseph's service to him, and few people were in a better position to help Joseph than he.

There are undoubtedly many people who have been influential for good in your life. The person who led you to salvation, Sunday school teachers who trained you, a friend who was always available when you needed someone to talk with—the list will get long if you ask the Lord to bring to mind the people who have helped you in the past.

We can show our gratitude to such people by praying for them, by returning favors when they need help, or even just spending time with them in loneliness. Ask the Lord to remind you of such people and to show you how you can return His love to them.

Whatever the Lord gives you to do, do it with all your might.

Joseph demonstrated this principle by carrying out every task with vigor and diligence. Most of us will never rise to second in command of a powerful nation—but then again, most of us will also not languish in prison for years under a false accusation. In both of these positions, Joseph carried out his work with all his might.

This is an excellent example of what the Lord calls His people to do. Whatever job He gives you, do it with the attitude that you are serving God directly, rather than men. The Scriptures confirm this counsel: "Whatever your hand finds to do, do it with your might; for there is no work or device or knowledge or wisdom in the grave where you are going" (Ecclesiastes 9:10). "And whatever you do, do it heartily, as to the Lord and not to men, knowing that from the Lord you will receive the reward of the inheritance; for you serve the Lord Christ" (Colossians 3:23–24).

⤳ DIGGING DEEPER ⤳

5. *What motivated Joseph to serve the butler and baker without grumbling?*

6. *Why did the captain of the guard give Joseph responsibility for the chief butler and chief baker? What did this reveal about Joseph's character?*

7. *Why did Joseph say that the interpretation of dreams belongs to God? What does this reveal about his faith?*

8. What does it mean to do something "as to the Lord and not to men"? What difference can such an attitude make in your performance at work? At home? At church?

↪ Taking It Personally ↩

9. Make a list below of people who have helped you in the past; then ask the Lord to show you how you can be of help to them in the future.

10. What jobs has the Lord given you in the coming week? How can you fulfill those responsibilities as to the Lord, rather than to men?

9
JACOB

⤳ HISTORICAL BACKGROUND ⤳

We are now at the end of Jacob's life, when he and his family have been living in Egypt under Joseph's care for a period of years. Jacob has grown frail, and his eyesight has failed. He senses that his days are growing short, and he wants to pass on his fatherly blessing to his children.

It is interesting that he begins solely with the sons of Joseph, before moving on to bless his own sons. Part of this first blessing is to adopt Joseph's sons as his own, rather than to view them as his grandsons. This is a mark of very high favor and esteem upon Joseph, since it confers upon his sons the full inheritance rights of Joseph and his brothers. It effectively triples Joseph's family inheritance by conferring a share upon his sons as well as himself.

Jacob then calls his twelve sons together and pronounces his blessing upon each individually. These blessings, however, are not simple benedictions; they are specific prophecies concerning the future tribes of Israel, the future descendants of each son. Jacob is blind, but he sees each son with a true and accurate vision, recognizing their strengths and weaknesses, their sins and areas of obedience. His words of prophecy will be fulfilled in the later history of the nation of Israel.

⤳ READING GENESIS 48:1–20 ⤳

JACOB ADOPTS TWO SONS: *Jacob has Joseph present his two sons, Ephraim and Manasseh, before him—and he adopts them as his own sons.*

1. AFTER THESE THINGS: Jacob and his entire family had been living in Egypt for some time, while Joseph was seated at Pharaoh's right hand.

MANASSEH AND EPHRAIM: These were Joseph's sons, born in Egypt. Manasseh means "causes [me] to forget." Ephraim means "double fruit." Manasseh was the older of the boys.

3. God Almighty appeared to me at Luz: See Genesis 28.

5. your two sons . . . are mine: Jacob adopted Joseph's two sons, Manasseh and Ephraim, as his own, elevating them to the status of firstborn sons rather than grandsons. He gave Ephraim the full birthright that would have fallen to Reuben, had he not committed his grievous sin.

6. Your offspring whom you beget after them shall be yours: That is, Joseph's future children would receive their inheritance from him; his third son would be treated as his firstborn, and so forth.

8. Who are these?: It is possible that Jacob was remembering the terrible trick he had played on his own blind father, pretending to be his older brother, Esau, in order to receive Esau's inheritance. (See Genesis 27.)

11. God has also shown me your offspring: Jacob recognized that God's hand had been guiding all the events in his life, even during the times when it appeared as though the Lord had abandoned him. God had led him through times of sorrow, yet in the end He blessed Jacob more greatly than he could have imagined.

Jacob Blesses His New Sons: *Jacob then places his hands of blessing upon Ephraim and Manasseh—but he deliberately reverses their birth order.*

13. Ephraim with his right hand toward Israel's left hand: Joseph attempted to arrange things so that the blessing of Jacob would be properly administered—according to human expectations. But God's will always overrides the efforts of mankind, and it was in God's plan to give the firstborn status to the younger son—as He had done with Jacob as well.

14. guiding his hands knowingly: Jacob deliberately crossed his hands, placing his right hand on the younger son and reversing the arrangement that Joseph anticipated. Thus, Jacob's blessing became a word of prophecy concerning Ephraim, anticipating that Ephraim would become the more influential of the two sons. The name Ephraim eventually became a substitute name for the nation of Israel. (See, for example, Isaiah 7.)

16. who has redeemed me from all evil: This is the first mention in Scripture of God as Redeemer, Deliverer, or Savior.

17. it displeased him: As we have seen in previous studies, the birthright of the firstborn son included the father's greatest blessing, as well as a larger share in the inheritance. The Lord, however, sometimes changed the order of precedence, as He did here and also in Jacob's case.

19. his younger brother shall be greater: Ephraim did indeed become the dominant tribe of the ten northern tribes of Israel.

⌁ READING GENESIS 49:1–28 ⌁

JACOB BLESSES HIS OWN SONS: *Sometime later, Jacob calls his own sons before him and blesses each. His words are prophecies concerning the future tribes of Israel.*

1. JACOB CALLED HIS SONS: Jacob had finished blessing the sons of Joseph and officially adopting them as his own sons. Now he called together all his sons to pronounce upon them his final words of blessing and prophecy. This section is highly poetic, and portrays the future history of the tribes that will descend from each son. The order of blessing does not follow any discernible pattern.

3. REUBEN, YOU ARE MY FIRSTBORN: Jacob began his blessing with his firstborn son, which would ordinarily have been natural. But in this case, he started by stating plainly that his firstborn son had lost the rights of the firstborn, due to his grievous sin.

MY MIGHT AND THE BEGINNING OF MY STRENGTH: In this heartbreaking statement, Jacob reminded Reuben what special blessings and influence were once his by right—all of which he had forever lost through sin. He had followed the pattern of Esau, who gave up his own birthright in exchange for a bowl of soup. (See Genesis 25.)

4. UNSTABLE AS WATER: The Hebrew phrase is literally "frothy water." Reuben was like a pot of boiling water—dangerous and unstable.

YOU WENT UP TO YOUR FATHER'S BED: See Genesis 35:22.

5. SIMEON AND LEVI ARE BROTHERS: That is, they are two of a kind.

INSTRUMENTS OF CRUELTY ARE IN THEIR DWELLING PLACE: The brothers had plundered the Hivites after slaughtering the family of Shechem and probably still had some of that plunder in their possession. (See Genesis 34.)

7. DIVIDE . . . SCATTER: Simeon eventually became the smallest tribe in Israel (Numbers 26:14) and eventually shared territory with Judah (Joshua 19:1–9). His descendants were omitted from Moses' blessing (Deuteronomy 33). Levi was scattered throughout Israel in the sense that his descendants did not receive any part of the promised land. Yet the Lord showed His grace to Levi's descendants when they remained loyal to Him (Exodus 32:26) by making them the priestly tribe in Israel. The Levites were the only people in Israel who could become priests—and as such, they were spread throughout the nation, never owning land.

8. JUDAH, YOU ARE HE WHOM YOUR BROTHERS SHALL PRAISE: This prophecy finds its ultimate fulfillment in Jesus, whose human lineage was descended through Judah.

YOUR FATHER'S CHILDREN SHALL BOW DOWN BEFORE YOU: This was fulfilled in David, Solomon, and their dynasty—Israel's great kings. It will ultimately be fulfilled, however, in Christ, before whom *every* knee shall bow.

10. Until Shiloh comes: This probably refers to Christ, who is called the "Lion of the Tribe of Judah" (Revelation 5:5).

11. Binding his donkey to the vine: This poetically describes a time of great prosperity, when people will tie a donkey to a choice vine and allow it to eat freely because of the abundance. Wine will be as plentiful as water, and people will enjoy good health and contentment (verse 12, "eyes . . . darker than wine; teeth whiter than milk"). This is probably a prophecy concerning the millennial kingdom of Christ.

Zebulun through Dan: *Jacob utters words of prophecy concerning the remaining tribes of Israel, many of which are fulfilled in the time of the judges.*

13. A haven for ships: The descendants of Zebulun did not live near the Mediterranean Sea, but their territory benefited from an important trade route that was used by sea traders in Canaan.

14. A strong donkey: The descendants of Issachar were a strong and industrious tribe. The name Issachar means "man of wages."

16. Dan shall judge his people: This was fulfilled in the period of the judges—including the notable Samson. The name Dan means "judge."

17. Bites the horse's heels: This prophecy probably points to Samson, at the very least, whose exploits caused the Philistines to rise up against the people of Israel, leading to the nation's finally taking control of Canaan under King David.

18. I have waited for your salvation, O Lord: Jacob's impassioned cry expressed hope for the tribe of Dan when salvation came to Israel—but Dan was ultimately omitted from the list of tribes in Revelation 7:4–8.

20. He shall yield royal dainties: The tribe of Asher settled in the agriculturally rich coastal region north of Carmel. They provided gourmet delights for the kings of Israel.

21. A deer let loose: The speed and agility of a deer marked the military prowess of the tribe of Naphtali. (See Judges 4:6, 5:18.)

He uses beautiful words: The song of Deborah and Barak demonstrates the tribe's eloquence (Judges 5).

23. Archers have bitterly grieved him: We have seen already how Joseph's life was filled with enemies, people even dear to him who sought his harm—yet Joseph "remained in strength . . . by the hands of the Mighty God."

27. Benjamin is a ravenous wolf: The warlike nature of the small tribe of Benjamin became well-known, as exhibited in their archers and slingers. (See, for example, Judges 20:15–16.)

⌒ FIRST IMPRESSIONS ⌒

1. How did God's blessings far exceed Jacob's expectations? How did God more than make up for the sufferings Jacob had experienced?

2. What stands out to you in the blessings of Jacob on his sons? What themes do you find there?

3. *If you were to choose one of the blessings on Jacob's sons, which would it be? Why?*

4. *Why is the blessing on Judah so significant? How does his blessing point to the coming of Jesus, the Messiah?*

⌁ Some Key Principles ⌁

Christians are adopted as sons of God, through Christ Jesus.

Jacob adopted Joseph's two sons as his own, and they received a full share of Israel's inheritance along with their father, Joseph. In an extended sense, this provides us a small picture of God's great plan of adoption, establishing each man and woman who accepts His Son's salvation as a child of God.

The picture is imperfect, however, because Joseph's sons were still part of Jacob's family—while we had no part in the family of God apart from Christ. We had no hope of seeing God's face, never mind any hope of inheriting eternal life in His presence. But His Son Jesus has shared with us His own inheritance, making us part of the family of God and children who have full access to the Father.

"When the fullness of the time had come, God sent forth His Son, born of a woman, born under the law, to redeem those who were under the law, that we might receive the adoption as sons. And because you are sons, God has sent forth the Spirit of His Son into your hearts, crying out, 'Abba, Father!' Therefore you are no longer a slave but a son, and if a son, then an heir of God through Christ" (Galatians 4:4–7).

God knows the truth about our character.

Jacob's blessings on his sons can seem startling in their frankness, but he was speaking truth about the sons' characters. He did not gloss over the sins of Reuben or Simeon, yet he also saw areas of strength and virtue. He spoke truth that sometimes hurt, and sometimes encouraged.

The Lord also sees the truth about our lives, the areas of sin and weakness as well as the areas of strength and obedience. God is no respecter of persons; He does not play favorites. The Lord's perspective on our character is the only *true* perspective, whatever other people may think.

There are times when we might think that a character flaw does not show to others; perhaps we have even blinded ourselves to it. But the Lord still sees what is true. Conversely, others may never know of the small areas of obedience and faithfulness that are done in secret—but the Lord knows. We are wise to remember that His evaluation of our lives is ultimately the only one that matters.

God sees His children through the blood of Christ.

The other side of the previous principle is vital to remember: God looks upon His children through the blood of Christ, and He sees us as spotless and immeasurably precious. When the Father looks upon us, He, in fact, sees His Son—and we are "accepted in the Beloved" (Ephesians 1:6).

We have been redeemed from sin, yet we are still sinful human beings while in this life. The Lord does see the sinfulness in our lives, yet He ultimately views us as His adopted sons—full heirs of all the promises of Christ. Our sinfulness does not negate our righteous standing before God, and we can never lose our adoption into His family.

"If we walk in the light as He is in the light, we have fellowship with one another, and the blood of Jesus Christ His Son cleanses us from all sin. If we say that we have no sin, we deceive ourselves, and the truth is not in us. [But if] we confess our sins, He is faithful and just to forgive us our sins and to cleanse us from all unrighteousness" (1 John 1:7–9).

5. Why did Jacob adopt Joseph's sons? What privileges did this adoption confer upon them?

6. What effects did sinful behavior have upon future generations in Jacob's family? What effects did godly character have on future generations?

7. Why did God "divide" and "scatter" the descendants of Simeon and Levi? Why was this a just inheritance for those brothers?

8. How does God show His grace and mercy in these blessings? How does He show His justice?

↜ TAKING IT PERSONALLY ↝

9. Do you think of yourself as an adopted son of God? How might this attitude influence your life in the coming week?

10. What is more important to your self-evaluation: the opinions of others, or the opinion of God? How does this play out in your daily life?

Section 3:

Themes

In This Section:

~ 10 ~
THE SOVEREIGNTY OF GOD

ᴧ THEMATIC BACKGROUND ᴧ

Joseph's life was filled with events that seemed arbitrary and out of his control. Indeed, most of those events *were* out of his control—but they were *not* out of God's control, nor were they random. The Lord had a large-scale plan to take His chosen nation, the descendants of Israel, into Egypt, and that plan included sending Joseph ahead of the family to prepare a place for them.

God's larger plan was to bring a Redeemer into the world through the lineage of Abraham, and to have Him ascend into heaven to prepare an eternal home for His children. And He has been unfolding this plan from before the foundation of the world (see Ephesians 1). He has used all sorts of events and people throughout history to bring this plan to fruition, and those events and people include things that were evil in themselves.

We will see this in Joseph's life in particular. God had planned that Joseph should go into Egypt ahead of his family and rise to prominence in Pharaoh's court. But Joseph also needed to learn certain skills and character traits to prepare him for that role, and the Lord knew exactly where he could best learn those lessons. Joseph's brothers, meanwhile, thought they could thwart God's promises to place them under Joseph's authority, and they set about to do some very wicked things to their brother. But God used those evil deeds to further His own good plan.

ᴧ READING GENESIS 37:5–11 ᴧ

JOSEPH'S DREAMS: *The Lord gave Joseph two prophetic dreams that foretold of events far in the future. These dreams were promises from God, and He always keeps His promises.*

5. JOSEPH HAD A DREAM: Before Joseph's long ordeal even began, the Lord gave Joseph a prophecy of things to come in the future. As Joseph went through a variety of terrible setbacks and found himself in apparently hopeless situations, he could look back upon the dreams and find encouragement in the knowledge that God was in control. In the same way, God's people today can find encouragement in the promises of God's Word.

THEY HATED HIM EVEN MORE: Joseph's brothers deliberately set themselves to oppose the plan of God in Joseph's life. They plotted to murder him, then sold him into slavery instead, saying to one another, "We shall see what will become of his dreams!" But God's plans cannot be thwarted by the wickedness of men, and we will see that He used the brothers' sin to actually advance the very plan they sought to frustrate.

7. MY SHEAF AROSE: As we have seen in previous studies, Joseph's prophetic dreams did in fact come to pass when he was elevated to a position of high authority in Egypt.

9. HE DREAMED STILL ANOTHER DREAM: It is significant that Joseph had two dreams rather than one. In the first dream, his brothers bowed themselves before him; in the second dream, his entire family bowed. This was fulfilled in the two stages of his family's move to Egypt. First his brothers came for food and bowed before him. After returning to Canaan several times, his entire family finally came and knelt before him. The Lord had every step planned out in advance, and the conspiracies of men could not prevent its fulfillment.

11. HIS BROTHERS ENVIED HIM: Here we are told the true motives behind his brothers' plot to murder him: they envied God's plan for his life. Yet the Lord has a glorious plan for each of His children, and we are unwise when we focus on what He has done for someone else.

⤳ READING GENESIS 39:19–23 ⤳

FALSELY ACCUSED: *Joseph rose to prominence in the household of Potiphar, and he might have been content in that position indefinitely. But God had other plans.*

19. HIS MASTER: That is, Potiphar. Potiphar's wife falsely accused Joseph of attempted rape after Joseph repeatedly refused her advances.

HIS ANGER WAS AROUSED: Potiphar's anger was justified if he truly believed what his wife told him. Nevertheless, his anger could not frustrate the Lord's plans for Joseph's life; in fact, Potiphar inadvertently furthered God's plan.

20. PUT HIM INTO THE PRISON: From a human perspective, this must have seemed a dead end for Joseph. He was a mere slave, the lowest class of humanity in a foreign land, with no friends or family to assist him. But the Lord wanted him in that specific prison at that specific time because He had a very specific task for him to perform there. Even when circumstances seem completely hopeless and out of control, God is completely *in* control and we have the glorious hope of His faithfulness.

A PLACE WHERE THE KING'S PRISONERS WERE CONFINED: If Joseph had not been sent to this particular prison, he would not have met Pharaoh's chief butler—yet Joseph did not know that at the time. When we trust God's sovereignty, He uses us for His purposes wherever we are.

21. THE LORD WAS WITH JOSEPH AND SHOWED HIM MERCY: Even in the midst of seemingly hopeless circumstances, the Lord shows us His mercy and faithfulness. Our job is to be looking for evidences of His presence. When we focus on God's sovereignty in our lives, we will see that He is working all things together for His glory, and we will be encouraged—even in the darkest hours.

23. BECAUSE THE LORD WAS WITH HIM: We have spent time in previous studies looking at the ways in which Joseph's attitude and behavior made him available for whatever the Lord had in store. But it is important to remember that every element of Joseph's story was under the Lord's control. Joseph did not find favor in the eyes of the prison warden simply because he was a diligent worker; he found favor because the Lord caused it to happen.

⤳ READING GENESIS 40:1–6, 23 ⤝

THE RIGHT PLACE AT THE RIGHT TIME: *Joseph needed to spend time in prison so that he could meet the chief butler. The Lord worked out details in his life—and the lives of others—for His purpose.*

1. THE BUTLER AND THE BAKER OF THE KING OF EGYPT OFFENDED THEIR LORD: God was in control of all events in the lives of all men, including those who did not acknowledge Him as Lord. It was part of God's plan that these two men should wind up in prison at this very time because He was at work in *their* lives as well as in Joseph's life. We do not know the biographies of the chief butler and chief baker, but we do know that the sovereign Lord chose to place them in prison. He was working out a plan for Joseph and for Jacob's entire family, but He was also working out His plans for these two men. God is absolutely sovereign in all affairs of all people.

2. PHARAOH WAS ANGRY WITH HIS TWO OFFICERS: This presents us with the flip side of God's sovereignty: the free will of mankind. The chief baker apparently had committed some crime against Pharaoh, since he ended up being executed. The Lord permits men and women to make their own choices—even when our choices lead to bad consequences. He permitted Adam to eat the forbidden fruit (Genesis 3), even though that decision led to sin and death entering the world. Mankind has the freedom to make choices; but those choices never frustrate God's sovereign purposes.

3. HE PUT THEM IN . . . THE PLACE WHERE JOSEPH WAS CONFINED: If Joseph had not been falsely accused by Potiphar's wife, he would not have been in the prison at this time. If the chief butler and chief baker had not angered Pharaoh, *they* would not have been in prison at this time. Indeed, if Joseph's brothers had not sold him into slavery, he would not have been in Egypt at all. In all these events, we see the sovereign will of God working through circumstances and men's actions—even wicked actions—to bring about His perfect plan.

5. THE BUTLER AND THE BAKER OF THE KING OF EGYPT . . . HAD A DREAM: The Lord used Joseph's dreams to provide him with encouragement and hope during times of despair, but He also used them to prepare him for this very day. In the same way, the Lord often sends experiences into our lives that prepare us for some future task—even though we may have no idea at the time what we are being prepared for.

23. THE CHIEF BUTLER DID NOT REMEMBER JOSEPH: This must have been a crushing blow to Joseph. He may have been filled with a sudden hope when he made such an important friend in the chief butler. He might have even thought that he could see how the Lord was going to work things together to free him from the prison by having the chief butler speak on his behalf to Pharaoh. Imagine his disappointment when it didn't work out! The long process of realizing that he'd been forgotten, each day his hope dwindling a little more, must have been very painful for Joseph. What's worse, he probably remained in prison for a couple of years after the chief butler had left, and it probably seemed to him at the time that he would spend the rest of his life there. He might even have wondered whether he had misinterpreted his prophetic dreams years before. But God had given him a promise, and He always keeps His promises.

ᴧ READING GENESIS 50:14–21 ᴧ

GOD MEANT IT FOR GOOD: *Joseph could have become discouraged and bitter at any point along a lifetime of disappointments and undeserved evil. But his focus was always on God's sovereignty.*

14. AFTER HE HAD BURIED HIS FATHER: We now zoom forward several years to the time when Joseph's entire family were living in Egypt. Jacob died and was buried in Canaan, and the family returned to their new homes in Goshen.

15. PERHAPS JOSEPH WILL HATE US: Joseph's brothers suddenly began to wonder whether Joseph had been kind to them solely to please their father. With him out of the way, would Joseph now remember all the evil they had done to him years before? Their sin against their brother was now coming back in the form of fear and false expectations, as they expected Joseph to behave toward them as they had behaved toward him.

FOR ALL THE EVIL WHICH WE DID TO HIM: Here we see that the brothers had indeed repented of their sins toward Joseph, as they recognized and freely confessed their wicked deeds. We will look at this further in Study 11.

17. JOSEPH WEPT WHEN THEY SPOKE TO HIM: This is a deeply moving passage, and we can understand the mixture of grief and joy Joseph must have felt. He was joyful that his brothers had repented, but grieved that they did not understand how much he loved them.

19. AM I IN THE PLACE OF GOD? : Joseph recognized that everything he'd experienced was under the direct control of God. The Lord had moved him from his father's family into slavery, from slavery into prison, and from prison to the house of Pharaoh—specifically because He had a plan for Jacob's descendants. Joseph realized that God was unfolding His plan for His people—a plan that extended far beyond the life of Jacob's immediate family—and he understood that his brothers' actions were used by God as part of that plan.

20. YOU MEANT EVIL AGAINST ME; BUT GOD MEANT IT FOR GOOD: Here is the crux of Joseph's attitude toward the many evils that were done against him: you meant it for evil, but God meant it for good. When we imitate this attitude, we spare ourselves a great deal of suffering during times of hardship, and we can fully cooperate with whatever plan the Lord is unfolding through our lives.

TO SAVE MANY PEOPLE ALIVE: Joseph also recognized that God's plan for his life was merely part of a larger plan for the entire family. Indeed, it was a small part of God's huge scheme for making redemption available to the entire human race. The Lord does work out the details of our lives for our own blessing, making us more and more like His Son, but His plans also extend far beyond our immediate lives to include others around us, and future generations as well. The sovereignty of God is too large for the human mind to comprehend.

↳ First Impressions ↲

1. Trace God's hand of sovereignty throughout the events in Joseph's life. How did God use circumstances to further His plan? How did He use people?

2. If you had been in Joseph's place, how would you have felt about the prophetic dreams of your youth?

3. How did Joseph's brothers show that they didn't understand God's sovereignty? What finally helped them learn that lesson?

4. *Why did Joseph repeatedly rise to positions of responsibility? How did these events demonstrate God's sovereignty?*

↵ Some Key Principles ↵

God is in control of all events in our lives, including times of suffering.

Joseph may have wondered at times whether there was any meaning or plan behind the events in his life. From a human perspective, those events certainly seem random at best. He had prophetic dreams promising that he would become an elevated ruler—and was almost immediately sold into slavery. He gained some ground serving in the house of Potiphar, then found himself thrown into prison with no apparent hope of release.

But in retrospect, God's hand of guidance could clearly be seen at each step along the way. The hard part is that we don't have that information at the time of hardship; God does not tell us exactly how He plans to use each event of our lives. He instead calls us to have faith in the fact that He *will* use those events to His glory, and it is that faith that can help us endure times of trial: "Now He who searches the hearts knows what the mind of the Spirit is, because He makes intercession for the saints according to the will of God. And we know that all things work together for good to those who love God, to those who are the called according to His purpose" (Romans 8:27–28).

The actions of men cannot frustrate the purposes of God.

Joseph's brothers envied the plans God had for him, and they conspired together to frustrate those plans. They deliberately set out to prevent him from ruling over them, first by planning to murder him and then by selling him into slavery. From a human perspective, it would certainly seem that God's plans had been thwarted when Joseph was led away in chains.

It turned out, however, that their wicked deeds merely advanced God's plan for Joseph's life. Joseph and his family could not see that at the time, but God knew exactly where He wanted Joseph at each step of the way, and what lessons Joseph would need to prepare him for his future task as ruler in Egypt. Potiphar's wife probably thought that she had effectively destroyed Joseph for scorning her advances, but God knew that Joseph needed to be in prison at that particular moment.

Years later, Joseph could look back on his brothers' treachery and declare that they meant it for evil, but God had intended it for good. God's good plans for our lives cannot be thwarted by the evil intentions of others. "If God is for us, who can be against us?" (Romans 8:31)

We do have the freedom to choose whether or not to obey.

God does not erase our ability to make choices by imposing His sovereign will over our decisions. He promised Jacob's family that Joseph would one day rule over them, but He did not force the family to honor that promise—He did not prevent the brothers from conspiring against Joseph. He told Adam that eating a certain fruit would bring death into the world, but He did not prevent Adam from eating that fruit. In His sovereign will, He had already made plans to redeem mankind from sin and death, but He still permitted Adam to choose for himself whether or not to obey.

Joseph's brothers did not like the plan that God had promised, and they actively tried to oppose it. We may not consciously be trying to circumvent the Lord's plan for our lives, but that is exactly what we are attempting whenever we deliberately disobey His Word. God's plan cannot be thwarted, and we only hurt ourselves when we disobey.

But we enable His fullest blessings in our lives whenever we submissively cooperate with His work.

5. What events in Joseph's life might have brought him to despair? Why did he not despair?

6. Why did Joseph continually trust in the sovereignty of God? What kept his faith alive?

7. When have you experienced a time of suffering that seemed completely random? How did God show you that He was in control?

8. When has another person done something deliberately evil to you? How did God use that for His glory?

↳ Taking It Personally ↲

9. What is God doing in your life today under His sovereign plan? Are you cooperating with Him, or fighting against Him?

10. In what areas of your life are you making obedient choices that glorify God? In what areas do your choices need to change?

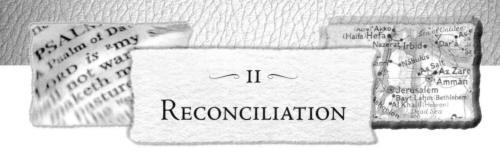

~ II ~

RECONCILIATION

⮑ THEMATIC BACKGROUND ⮐

The word *reconciliation* comes from a Latin word meaning "to become physically united once again." It suggests that something—a teacup, for example—has been broken in two and needs to be joined together again. This is a perfect word picture of the process of reconciliation: to rejoin two people who have been broken apart.

Joseph's family was shattered when his brothers sold him into slavery and told their father that he was dead. One of Joseph's foremost desires would have been to reunite his family—to pick up the pieces and glue them back into a single harmonious family. And this was precisely what God desired, as well.

The Lord calls His people to be reconciled together, to work constantly at forgiving one another and "gluing together" fractured relationships. He has made His children into a single family, the unified body of Christ, and any division within that body is as painful as a broken bone. The devil works to divide Christians, but the Holy Spirit works through us to bring harmony and reconciliation.

In this study, we will examine how Joseph worked to reunite his family, and we will look for principles that can help us in the work of reconciliation.

⮑ READING GENESIS 42:1–24 ⮐

THE BROTHERS HEAD TO EGYPT: *We return to the time of the famine, when Jacob sent his sons to Egypt to buy food. This is the beginning of family reconciliation.*

1. THERE WAS GRAIN IN EGYPT: The famine had grown so severe that there was no food anywhere in Canaan. But the Lord had provided enough to feed Egypt and Canaan by sending Joseph ahead to make preparations.

3. JOSEPH'S TEN BROTHERS WENT DOWN TO BUY GRAIN IN EGYPT: This, too, was the Lord's plan being worked out, as He intended that the same brothers who sold Joseph into slavery should follow in his footsteps. The Lord's intention was to bring about reconciliation within Jacob's family.

4. Joseph's brother Benjamin: Benjamin and Joseph were both born through Rachel. Jacob had not forgotten the tragic loss of Joseph, and he had no intention of losing his other favorite son.

5. among those who journeyed: People were traveling to Egypt from all over Canaan, and probably beyond, because there was no food anywhere else. Joseph's brothers were merely a few men within a huge crowd that descended upon Egypt; it took a miracle from the Lord for them even to encounter Joseph. This may also have given them a small taste of what it felt like to be sold into slavery.

Bowing Before Joseph: *Now, after twenty-two years, Joseph's prophetic dreams start to be fulfilled, as his brothers bow before him.*

6. Joseph's brothers came: It is possible that Joseph sat in attendance each day, perhaps elevated above the crowds. It may also have been the Lord's direct intervention to bring him to the market at just the right time for his brothers' appearance. Either way, this was no coincidence, for the Lord had foretold this very event many years earlier.

and bowed down before him: Here at last we find the literal fulfillment of Joseph's first dream (Genesis 37:5–10), as his brothers bow before him. His second dream had yet to be fulfilled, in which his entire family bowed before him.

7. he acted as a stranger to them: This indeed was the case, since Joseph left Canaan at age seventeen and was now thirty-nine. His entire youth was spent in Egypt, mostly in captivity, and his brothers could not truly say that they knew him anymore.

spoke roughly to them: This was the beginning of Joseph's plan of reconciliation, but it had to start with some rough treatment. It was far less rough than the treatment his brothers had afforded him many years earlier, yet Joseph also could not pretend that the betrayal and attempted murder had never happened.

8. they did not recognize him: This is humorous in its understatement. The brothers probably assumed that Joseph was dead by this time. He had been a seventeen-year old stripling when they had last seen him, and he was now grown to a strong, commanding adult. He had been an uneducated shepherd lad, and now he stood before them in full splendor as the head of all Egypt. Joseph had been transformed from a rustic nomad—thought to be dead by his family—into one of the most powerful men on earth. It is hardly surprising that the brothers did not recognize him!

Refreshing Their Memories: *Joseph immediately sets about addressing the sins his brothers committed against him, working always toward reconciliation rather than revenge.*

9. You are spies: He made this accusation as an excuse to speak to them more closely and in private as an interrogator. Joseph wanted to test his brothers' hearts to find out whether they had repented of their wickedness toward him, and he also longed for news of his father and brother Benjamin.

10. No, my lord, but your servants . . . : This is further fulfillment of the Lord's prophecies through Joseph's dream. "And his brothers said to him, 'Shall you indeed reign over us? Or shall you indeed have dominion over us?' " (Genesis 37:8). Here at last the brothers acknowledged—without even realizing it—that their brother Joseph did indeed have dominion over them. It was important to the family's reconciliation that the brothers confess openly that the Lord's prophecies had been fulfilled.

11. your servants are not spies: The brothers had come to Egypt in all innocence, not expecting any trouble but merely wanting to buy food, as indeed everyone else in Canaan was doing. But to their dismay, they found themselves unexpectedly in grave danger. At this charge, they would have begun to fear for their lives, as spies would certainly have been put to death. In all this, they were merely experiencing a small portion of what they had done to Joseph.

13. and one is no more: This statement revealed several things to Joseph. It showed that the brothers had long since given him up for dead, but it also showed that their consciences were still alive to what they had done. It did not take much to bring Joseph's "death" into the conversation, and this showed that there was still hope for reconciliation.

Looking for Repentance: *Joseph wanted to know that his brothers had repented of their sins against him, so he gave them an opportunity to demonstrate it.*

15. you shall be tested: This in fact was precisely what Joseph was doing: he was testing his brothers' hearts to find whether they had repented of their sins against him.

unless your youngest brother comes here: By focusing on Benjamin, Joseph actually forced his brothers to relive some of the events of the past, when they had betrayed their father's favorite son. He was placing them in a position where they would have to determine how to treat Jacob's remaining favorite.

19. let one of your brothers be confined: Joseph had originally said that one brother would go to Canaan while nine remained, but here he reversed it. The latter plan was better for his purposes, as it forced the brothers to speak together on their way home, and Joseph was confident that the subject of his betrayal would figure into their conversation.

20. bring your youngest brother to me: Again, Joseph was forcing his brothers to address what they had done years before, giving them an opportunity to repent.

21. WE ARE TRULY GUILTY CONCERNING OUR BROTHER: Joseph could only offer the opportunity of repentance; he could not force his brothers to face their guilt. But the Spirit of God is always at work in His people, leading us to confess our sins and work toward reconciliation. That is precisely what was happening to Joseph's brothers here.

22. DID I NOT SPEAK TO YOU . . . ? : See Genesis 37:21. Reuben had been the only brother of the ten who had attempted to save Joseph's life. Nevertheless, he had joined with his brothers in deceiving Jacob after selling Joseph into slavery (37:31–32), and had done nothing to bring Joseph back from Egypt—yet here he was suggesting that his guilt had been less than his brothers. In the end, it would be Judah who came forth as the leader in the family.

24. HE TURNED HIMSELF AWAY FROM THEM AND WEPT: Joseph was not enjoying the process of putting his brothers through this anguish, but he felt that it was necessary if full reconciliation was to take place.

⌁ READING GENESIS 43:24–30 ⌁

A LONG-LOST BROTHER: *Joseph meets his brothers again, and this time Benjamin is with them. After twenty-two years, he can hardly believe his eyes.*

24. BROUGHT THE MEN INTO JOSEPH'S HOUSE: The brothers had gone home to Canaan, and were now returned to Egypt with Benjamin, as Joseph had commanded.

25. THEY WOULD EAT BREAD THERE: Joseph deliberately kept the brothers in private throughout this difficult process.

27. IS YOUR FATHER WELL? : At each step along the way, Joseph betrayed his deep longing to be reconciled with his family. His brothers did not know who he was, and he yearned to reach the point where he could be reunited with them as part of the family. It must have been a great joy to him to learn that his father was still alive.

28. PROSTRATED THEMSELVES: It is interesting to note how many times the brothers bowed before Joseph. This was more than fulfillment of Joseph's prophetic dreams; it was a sign that complete reconciliation had not yet taken place. Once the family was fully reconciled together, the brothers no longer needed to prostrate themselves before Joseph, for he would treat them as his brothers. The one exception to this came after Jacob's death, when the brothers fell into fear that Joseph would seek revenge.

29. IS THIS YOUR YOUNGER BROTHER? : It had been more than two decades since Joseph had seen Benjamin, who was just a boy when they were separated.

30. Joseph made haste: Joseph made forgiveness and reconciliation with his brothers a top priority, which is why he did not waste any time in testing them.

weep . . . wept: Joseph wept frequently throughout the reconciliation process. These were probably mixed tears: tears of sorrow over the many years of separation, mingled with tears of joy over the reunion.

⌒ Reading Genesis 45:1–15 ⌒

Fully Reconciled: *Joseph demonstrates the most important and final step in reconciliation: complete forgiveness.*

1. Joseph could not restrain himself: This took place immediately after Judah had offered himself in exchange for Benjamin's life, motivated by a concern for the grief of their father. (See Study 7.) Here at last, Joseph could see that Judah and his brothers had repented of their sin against him, and he was so moved by joy and yearning that he could no longer restrain his tears.

no one stood with him: Here Joseph demonstrated that reconciliation is a private matter, not to be shared with an audience.

Joseph made himself known to his brothers: Imagine the many powerful emotions that were surging in the breasts of the family at this moment. Joseph was overcome with joy at seeing his family again. Benjamin was probably overwhelmed with wonder to find that his long-dead brother was, in fact, alive—and a powerful ruler, besides. The other brothers probably felt a strong mixture of emotions, including awe at the fulfillment of Joseph's prophetic dreams, and fear to be at his mercy.

3. they were dismayed: Literally, they were alarmed—and terrified. They fully expected that Joseph would desire revenge for their crimes against him, and they recognized that he could exact that revenge with complete impunity. This allowed the brothers to experience the utter powerlessness and terror that Joseph had felt many years before. But in their fear, they did not understand the heart of their brother.

4. whom you sold into Egypt: True reconciliation requires honesty from all parties. Joseph did not downplay what his brothers had done, nor did he ignore their sin or try to gloss over it. They had sinned against him without cause, and all the brothers—including Joseph—needed to acknowledge that fact.

5. do not therefore be grieved or angry with yourselves: The step of honest confession and admission of past sins must be followed with the step of full forgiveness. Forgiveness includes relinquishing any "right" or desire for revenge, just as Joseph freely relinquished his legal right and authority to exact revenge on his brothers.

GOD SENT ME BEFORE YOU TO PRESERVE LIFE: Joseph recognized the sovereign hand of God, and he understood that the Lord was the one who had sent him to Egypt. He also appreciated the dichotomy of God's sovereignty versus man's free will, which we looked at in Study 10. He knew that the Lord had arranged circumstances and had used the deeds of men in order to further His own plans, but he also recognized that his brothers had sinned and needed to be reconciled with him.

15. AFTER THAT HIS BROTHERS TALKED WITH HIM: The family had been fully reconciled to one another, and they could once again speak together as brothers.

⌁ FIRST IMPRESSIONS ⌁

1. *If you had been in Joseph's place, how would you have treated your brothers?*

2. *If you had been in the brothers' place, how would you have reacted when Joseph revealed his true identity?*

3. Why did Joseph meet with his brothers in private? What does this teach about forgiveness and reconciliation?

4. What steps were involved for the brothers to confess and repent of their sins against Joseph? What experiences helped them in that process?

⌁ Some Key Principles ⌁

God's people should always be reconciled with one another.

Joseph never showed any inclination in his life to get revenge on his brothers, or on anyone else who wronged him. His desire was just the opposite: to be reunited in complete unity and love with his family. And the moment he had an opportunity, he set about working toward that reconciliation.

This is the example for all of God's people. We are to make reconciliation and forgiveness top priority in our lives. People do sin, and sometimes they will hurt us—intentionally or unintentionally, the pain is the same. Our job in such circumstances is to approach the person who has offended us—not in order to confront him with his sin, but to offer forgiveness and reconciliation. This principle works in both directions, whether we are the ones offended or the ones who gave offense.

"If you bring your gift to the altar, and there remember that your brother has something against you, leave your gift there before the altar, and go your way. First be reconciled to your brother, and then come and offer your gift" (Matthew 5:23–24).

Forgiveness can be offered by one party alone, but reconciliation requires mutual effort.

Joseph had forgiven his brothers for their sin long before he met them in Egypt. He had recognized that it was God's plan that he be in Egypt in order to provide food for many people, and he had no desire to avenge himself for any sins against him. He was able to forgive regardless of his brothers' response.

But he was not able to be fully reconciled with his family until his brothers acknowledged their sin and repented. This is a critical element in reconciliation: we must be willing to confess any action that might have hurt another person, and we must acknowledge that we have repented of that hurt—whether it was intentional or not.

This principle, like the previous one, works in both directions. We must be quick to be reconciled with others, regardless whether we are the offending party or the offended party. "Confess your trespasses to one another, and pray for one another, that you may be healed. The effective, fervent prayer of a righteous man avails much" (James 5:16).

Remember that God is in control of all our circumstances.

We have covered this point in previous studies, but it is important to reiterate here. Joseph found it much easier to forgive his brothers because he kept in mind that it was God's will for him to be in Egypt, regardless of what his brothers had intended. He lived with a constant recognition of God's sovereignty over the affairs of his life, and this enabled him to quickly forgive those who sinned against him.

Joseph's brothers had a somewhat more difficult task in being reconciled because they did not fully understand this important concept. When Jacob died, they immediately became afraid again, thinking that Joseph had complete power over their lives. But Joseph reminded them that he was not God, and that God alone had sovereignty.

When you are hurt by the sins of another person, remember Joseph's wise deduction: "You meant evil against me; but God meant it for good" (Genesis 50:20).

5. What things were required on Joseph's part to attain reconciliation? What was required on his brothers' part?

6. Why did Joseph test his brothers? If a brother or sister repents of a sin against you, should you "test" that repentance, or accept it at face value (see Matthew 18:21–22)?

7. Why did Joseph want to be reconciled in the first place? What did he gain from it? What did others gain?

8. How can you use this example to be reconciled with others in your own life?

↳ Taking It Personally ↲

9. Is there a relationship in your life that needs to be reconciled? What will you do this week to accomplish that?

10. Is there someone that you need to forgive? Do you need to ask forgiveness of someone else? What steps will you take today to gain or offer forgiveness?

Section 4:

Summary

Notes and Prayer Requests

12

Reviewing Key Principles

Looking Back

In the preceding eleven studies, we have looked closely at the family of Jacob and have seen both great weaknesses and great strengths. The characters we have examined were real people, just like us, who were confronted with life in a sinful world. Some of them remained steadfast through it all, faithful to the God they served. Others responded to their circumstances with sinful self-interest. But God worked in the life of each, no matter what his response.

Throughout these studies, we have seen a constant theme: God's sovereignty. We have learned that man does have freedom to choose obedience or disobedience, but no matter what his choice, God remains sovereign. Sometimes His people made terrible choices—actions that led to heartache and even disgrace. Yet every step of the way, God proved His faithfulness to His people, extending grace and reconciliation even to those who had committed terrible sins.

God wants to be reconciled with sinful people, and He commands His people to be reconciled with one another. A key element in this process is to remember that God is sovereign, and He controls every circumstance in our lives. So even if we are hurt by someone else, God remains in control and can, in fact, use our pain to make us better people.

Here are a few of the major themes we have found in our study of Jacob and his family. There are many more that we don't have room to reiterate, so take some time to review the earlier studies—or better still, to meditate upon the passages in Scripture that we have covered. Ask that the Holy Spirit give you wisdom and insight into His Word. He will not refuse.

Some Key Principles

God is in control of all our circumstances, even when things seem to be going wrong.

The Lord had told Abraham, many years before Joseph was born, that his descendants would go into Egypt for four hundred years (Genesis 15:13–14). It was His plan from the beginning that Joseph should lead his family into Egypt, and the events in these studies were part of that plan.

But the hand of God was not readily apparent in these events, particularly to the people who were living through them. Joseph probably did not sit rejoicing at the bottom of the pit, thrilled that God was sending him to Egypt to fulfill His prophecy to Abraham; it is much more likely that he was overcome with grief and fear, wondering what was going to happen next—wondering, indeed, whether or not he would be murdered by his own brothers.

Yet the Lord is completely sovereign over all things in our lives, and He has promised that He will always be faithful to His children. "And we know that all things work together for good to those who love God, to those who are the called according to His purpose" (Romans 8:28).

We are still responsible for our own actions.

The other side to the previous principle is that God's sovereignty does not exonerate us from our own responsibility. Joseph's brothers were fully responsible before God for attempting to murder him and for selling him into slavery.

The Lord can and does use the wicked actions of evil men to accomplish His holy purposes, because His plans cannot be thwarted by the conduct of human beings or even by Satan himself. But this is to the glory of God, not to the praise of wicked men. Joseph's brothers still had to answer for their deeds, even though God used those deeds to further His plans for Israel.

The good news is that the Lord also uses our obedience to further His purposes and bring glory to His name—and we grow in Christlikeness in the process. Joseph's responses to his brothers' deeds demonstrated this, and his life became a picture of the life of Christ.

Vengeance belongs to God, not to us.

Shechem's sin against Dinah brought disgrace upon her entire family, and her brothers were right to be angry. They were wrong, however, to take their own revenge upon the people of that city; in so doing, they were as guilty as Shechem for not controlling their own passions.

We all suffer at the hands of other people from time to time, and sometimes we can be called to suffer greatly. We must remember to view such sufferings as God's tools of purification and strengthening for us. Those who hate us are not permitted to cause evil in our lives unless God allows it—and when He does allow it, it is for a reason.

God's reasons for allowing His children to suffer are always intended to bring glory to His name. It may be that He is working to bring the wrongdoer to salvation, or perhaps He is simply making us more like Christ. Whether we can see a reason or not, we must never repay evil with evil. "Beloved, do not avenge yourselves, but rather give place to wrath; for it is written, 'Vengeance is Mine, I will repay,' says the Lord. Therefore 'If your enemy is hungry, feed him; if he is thirsty, give him a drink; for in so doing you will heap coals of fire on his head.' Do not be overcome by evil, but overcome evil with good" (Romans 12:19–21).

Do not try to simply endure strong temptation—run away!

Joseph was a healthy young man in his prime, cut off from family and friends and lonely in a foreign land. As such, the temptations of Potiphar's wife must have been powerful indeed. Yet Joseph demonstrated the right way to deal with such temptations: he fled! He refused to discuss the subject with the one who tempted him, refused even to be in her company. In fact, he evidently made a point of trying never to be alone in the house with her. When he did end up alone in her presence, it was by accident. What did he do in this dangerous predicament? He ran away—quite literally, even to the point of leaving his cloak in her hands.

Some situations require us to persevere in daily decisions to please our Father, but others can only be overcome by running away. "Be sober, be vigilant; because your adversary the devil walks about like a roaring lion, seeking whom he may devour. Resist him, steadfast in the faith, knowing that the same sufferings are experienced by your brotherhood in the world" (1 Peter 5:8–9). Sometimes, the best way to resist a roaring lion is to flee.

The Lord uses trials to prepare us for greater tasks.

Joseph suffered greatly when his brothers betrayed him, and later when Potiphar's wife falsely accused him. Yet these trials were *permitted* by God, even though it might have been hard for Joseph to see God's hand at the time. The Lord was, in fact, using those trials to strengthen Joseph's faith, and also to teach him very practical lessons that he would need later. Joseph had no idea that he would one day rule over all Egypt, and he consequently could not have prepared himself with the skills that would be required. Only the Lord knew those things, and He used disappointments and setbacks and slavery and imprisonment to train Joseph for the future.

We may never become world leaders in this life, but the Lord's plans for our future are still important in the eternal scheme. And the day will come when all of His people shall rule the world—in fact, we will rule with Him over all creation, for all eternity. He is preparing each of us now to be ready for that great role of leadership, and He uses every circumstance in our lives for that preparation—including suffering and hardship.

The Lord always provides for His people.

The famine and drought in Egypt and Canaan were very severe, and it is likely that many people died during that time. Yet all of Jacob's household survived—in fact, they more than survived; they thrived when the world around them was in want.

That famine did not catch God by surprise; He ordained it as part of His plan to move Israel into Egypt in preparation for their exodus into the promised land of Canaan. He saw all things that would transpire in the future, even to the end of time, and He had planned from before the beginning of time exactly how He would prove His faithfulness to His people.

Sometimes, however, His provision required some of His people to suffer. Joseph suffered grievously prior to being elevated to the leadership of Egypt, and it is likely that he wondered at times whether God had forgotten him. But the Lord had not forgotten Joseph, or any others in the family of Israel, and He proved His faithfulness by providing for all their needs. He never forgets His promises or His children.

Whatever the Lord gives you to do, do it with all your might.

Joseph demonstrated this principle by carrying out every task with vigor and diligence. Most of us will never rise to be second in command of a powerful nation—but then again, neither will most of us languish in prison for years, under a false accusation. In both of these positions, Joseph carried out his work with all his might.

This is an excellent example of what the Lord calls His people to do. Whatever job He gives you, do it with the attitude that you are serving God directly, rather than men.

"Whatever your hand finds to do, do it with your might; for there is no work or device or knowledge or wisdom in the grave where you are going" (Ecclesiastes 9:10). "And whatever you do, do it heartily, as to the Lord and not to men, knowing that from the Lord you will receive the reward of the inheritance; for you serve the Lord Christ" (Colossians 3:23–24).

God's people should always be reconciled with one another.

Joseph never showed any inclination in his life to get revenge on his brothers, or on anyone else who wronged him. His desire was just the opposite: to be reunited in complete unity and love with his family. And the moment he had an opportunity, he set about working toward that reconciliation.

This is the example for all of God's people. We are to make reconciliation and forgiveness a top priority in our lives. People do sin, and sometimes they will hurt us—deliberately or not, the pain is the same. Our job in such circumstances is to approach the person who has offended us—not in order to confront him with his sin, but to offer forgiveness and reconciliation. This principle works in both directions, whether we are the offended or the ones who gave offense.

"Therefore if you bring your gift to the altar, and there remember that your brother has something against you, leave your gift there before the altar, and go your way. First be reconciled to your brother, and then come and offer your gift" (Matthew 5:23–24).

∽ Digging Deeper ∼

1. What are some of the more important things that you have learned from these chapters of Genesis?

2. Which of the concepts or principles have you found most encouraging? Which have been most challenging?

3. What aspects of "walking with God" are you already doing in your life? Which areas need strengthening?

4. Which of the characters that we've studied have you felt the most attracted to? How might you emulate that person in your own life?

⤙ Taking It Personally ⤚

5. Have you taken a definite stand for Jesus Christ? Have you accepted His free gift of salvation? If not, what is preventing you from doing so?

6. What areas of your personal life have been most convicted during this study? What exact things will you do to address these convictions? Be specific.

7. What have you learned about the character of God during this study? How has this insight affected your worship or prayer life?

8. List below the specific things that you want to see God do in your life in the coming month. List also the things that you intend to change in your own life in that time. Return to this list in one month and hold yourself accountable to fulfill these things.

If you would like to continue in your study of the Old Testament, read the next title in this series: *The Exodus from Egypt: Moses and God's Mercy.*